Cont

Introduction

Barcelona is the largest and most exciting port city in the Mediterranean. It basks in a nest of hills in the northeast corner of Spain, with its back to Madrid and its eyes on the sea that gave it, in parts, a glorious past.

Down by the port

Formal, mercantile, medieval – the city's past reverberates in the dank canyons of the old town and in the vast dockyards that today form the maritime museum. Add to this a creativity of spirit that was responsible for some of the finest Romanesque art in the world as well as the great 19th-century *modernista*

A detail of the Columbus monument

buildings of Gaudí and others, and you arrive at a dazzling mix of old and new, a place that never lacks the courage of its convictions. Reticence and shyness are strangers here.

Spain's second city has for nearly two centuries been the industrial, money-making part of the country, though the textile industry that brought wealth to the early arts patrons such as Eusebi Güell declined significantly in the 1980s. It is still rich, however, producing 20 per cent of the country's GDP, and people continue to arrive from all over Spain looking for work. Its popular coasts – the Costa Brava to the north and Costa Daurada to the south – are also places where people come to find work.

Cultural Hothouse

From this vibrant background have come first-rate art and culture, from opera singers and film directors to painters, designers and architects, all of whom are accorded great respect. Its cultural institutions – the Picasso Museum, Liceu opera house, and museums of Romanesque and contemporary art – are world-class. Much of the entertainment is out in the streets, however, and few cities offer the visitor so much to see by doing nothing but simply wandering around.

The People

Two opposite poles are at work on the Catalan psyche. *Seny* is the sensibility that produces the bourgeois traditionalist who can be seen among the elegant crowd arriving in the Rambla for the latest offering at the Liceu opera. *Rauxa* is the impetuousness that has resulted in fits of church burning, and the creativity so suited to Surrealism. In Catalans these two elements are said to live side by side.

Catalan (*català, see pp24–5*) is the first language of the city and this sets it apart from other regions of Spain. This independence has been fought for down the centuries, and native *Barcelonans* are still likely still see themselves as Catalans first and Spaniards second.

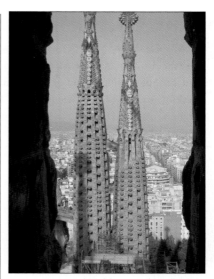

The Sagrada Família, Gaudí's greatest legacy

La Rambla, one of the most enjoyable streets in the world

When to Visit

The city is good for visiting year round. Winters can be cold but bright, with chilly evenings and an average temperature of 10°C (50°F). School summer holidays last three months and during July and August, when temperatures soar, families try to escape to the hills and the coasts, leaving the city to the breadwinners and to visitors. For anyone staying more than a few days, a trip to the coast provides a welcome break, and there are also many historical sites to see inland, from Montserrat monastery to Roman Tarragona, and from medieval towns to *cava* vineyards. The ideal months to visit are May and June, or September and October, when the full heat has left the sun and the sea is still warm enough to swim in.

The City

Hard by the sea and beneath two imposing hills, Barcelona has spread into the surrounding communities, scooping up a third of the population of Catalonia, the region over which it presides. Extending from the Pyrenees to the Mediterranean, it has an abundance of natural resources that have helped to make this city of merchants and manufacturers great.

Plaça del Pi, the old town

Barcelona is the capital of Catalonia, the region of northeast Spain that was conceived by the Francs in AD 850 as a buffer state against the ebbing tide of Muslims. Its founder was Guifré el Pelós (Wilfred the Hairy), the first Count of Barcelona, whose family ruled in an unbroken line for 500 years. Until 1659 the territory extended into France and as a result, with a language akin to Provençal or Langue d'Oc, it has sometimes felt more affinity with Paris than with Madrid, an upstart town set up in the centre of the peninsula in 1561 to unite the disparate regions of Spain. Rivalry between the two cities remains brisk.

Roman Foundations

Barcelona is at heart a Roman town. The Plaça St Jaume is where the forum stood and its foundations can be seen beneath the Palau Reial (*see pp46–7*). Roman walls are still visible by the cathedral and by the former royal palace, and it is easy to see how the city spread.

These walls proved insufficient by the 14th century when the nation was at the height of its expansion, and the medieval walls were built, encompassing the business quarter around the stock exchange and at first lining the Rambla, then encompassing the working district of El Raval. In the 19th century the

The Ajuntament, the city hall, in Plaça Sant Jaume where the Roman forum stood

population burst out of the walls altogether and the *modernista* Eixample ('extension', *see pp60–63*) was built.

Recent Developments

Decades of under-investment and neglect in the Franco years saved the city from the blight of any sixties' high-rise developments. When investment did come, it arrived in a magnificent rush for the 1992 Olympic Games, and the infrastructure was bulldozed into the 21st century with breathtaking panache, thanks to men of vision such as the architect Oriol Bohigas and the city mayor, Pasqual Maragall, a qualified town planner. Almost overnight, Barcelona was transformed.

It was as if the city had been waiting to awake. Ring roads went in, new Metro lines were established and the whole of the seafront, with the Olympic Port, were opened up, giving the city new icons such as the Hotel Arts, taller than any other building in Spain. Once the ball began to roll, it kept going, opening up new city spaces and looking up the coast past the Olympic developments towards 2004 when the Diagonal, the thoroughfare that runs at odds with the grid-like streets of the Eixample, finally reaches the sea and the new, invisible, city walls stretch all the way to the River Besòs.

The Metropolitan Area

The city reached its present boundaries of 97sq km (37sq miles) in 1929 and now has a population of 1.7 million. The metropolitan area, with an additional 2.3 million people, spreads out into surrounding towns and includes 164 municipalities and seven *comarques*. A *comarca* is a municipal area of Catalonia, ruled by a comarcal council. There are 41 altogether, divided among four provinces each named after its principal city: Barcelona, Girona, Lleida and Tarragona.

The Hills

Two hills look down on the city. By the sea is Montjuïc 213m (700ft) on which the castle sits overlooking the still active port and the sea, with funfairs and pleasure palaces tumbling around its feet. Inland is the other pleasure garden of Tibidabo 512m (1,680ft) and the Collserola hills, a hunting ground for boar and wild mushrooms. Dotted about in between are communities that have managed to maintain a village feel, such as Sarrià and Gràcia. Each district has its own flavour, its own shops, its own feast day.

THE RHYTHM OF LIFE

The city stirs late, especially downtown where shops and even some cafés do not open until 10am. Most Barcelonans live within easy commuting distance of the city and at 2pm they hurry home to lunch, leaving the city to siesta until 4pm when another rush hour fills the streets again.

In summer, to avoid the worst of the heat, office workers may labour straight through from 8am until 3pm, when they can take off for the beach or the cool of their homes. In the hottest month, August, some work places and factories close altogether.

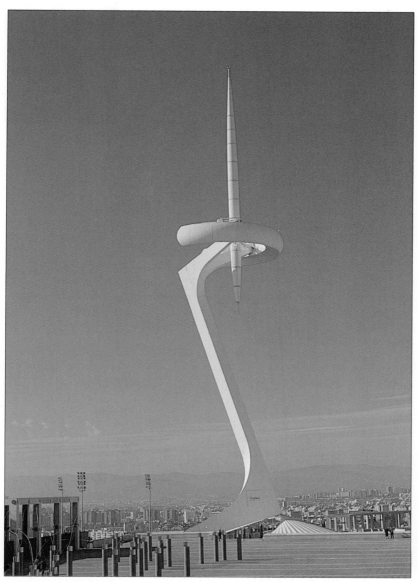

The Torre de Calatrava on Montjuïc, site of the 1992 Olympic Games

History

The royal palace

700 BC	First settlements by indigenous Iberians, the Laeitani.
300 BC	Carthaginians from southeast Spain under Hamil Barca take over the city, renaming it Barcino.
217 BC	After Barca's son, Hannibal, marches on Rome, the Romans respond by invading Spain, landing on the Costa Brava to start their conquest of the peninsula.
200 BC	Roman Barcelona established.
AD 476	After the fall of Rome, Visigoths fill the vacuum.
700	Moors cross from Africa and take over Spain, capturing Barcelona in 713. They are repulsed by the Francs who set up the *Marca Hispanica* ('Spanish March').
897	Death in battle of Guifré el Pelós, first Count of Barcelona.
988	Barcelona declared autonomous after the Moors are pushed back to the south.
1137	The House of Barcelona is joined with neighbouring Aragon through marriage.
Late 13th century	The House of Catalonia–Aragon becomes a dominant force in the Mediterranean.
1359	Establishment of *Corts Catalanes*, the nation's parliament.
1395	The *Jocs Florals*, troubadour poetry competitions, are introduced during a literary flowering.
1469	Ferdinand of Aragon marries Isabella of Castile (the Catholic Monarchs), uniting the two major houses of Spain.
1492	Moors expelled from Spain, Jews outlawed.

Columbus discovers America and returns to Barcelona with Carib Indians to be baptised in the cathedral. Trade with the New World is denied Barcelona, however, leading to its decline.

1659 The Treaty of the Pyrenees concludes the Thirty Years War between Spain and France, ceding all Catalan territories north of the Pyrenees to France.

1714 In the War of the Spanish Succession, Barcelona backs the House of Habsburg, but the Bourbons are victorious. After a 13-month siege, the city falls on 11 September (*La Diada*), a national day in Catalonia. The *Corts* are abolished, the language banned, and a citadel (La Ciutadella) is built to police the city.

1808 Barcelona is taken by Napoleonic troops in the War of Independence.

1814 After peace is restored in Europe, Barcelona flourishes, becoming the industrial powerhouse of Spain, introducing steam to power its textile mills.

1833 Start of the protracted Carlist Wars, instigated by the pretender, Don Carlos.

1835 Many religious houses closed and land redistributed.

1848 Mainland Spain's first train operates between Barcelona and Mataró.

1854–6 La Ciutadella is pulled down along with the city walls as the population explodes.

The magnificent façade of Santa Maria del Mar

1859	The *Renaixença* ('renaissance') of Catalan, with a revival of the *Jocs Florals*.
1860	The new city (Eixample) is designed by Ildefons Cerdà.
1888	The Universal Exhibition is held in the Parc de la Ciutadella, and the *modernista* style of architecture is celebrated.
1901–2	General strike by city workers.
1909	*Setmana Tràgica* ('tragic week'): widespread rioting and destruction of religious houses.
1923	Catalan aspirations thwarted by the dictatorship of Primo de Rivera.
1929	A second Universal Exhibition is held on Montjuïc, where the Poble Espanyol and other lasting architectural curiosities are built.
1931	Under the Second Republic Catalonia is granted its first statute of independence.
1936–9	The Spanish Civil War begins after Nationalist

insurgents under General Franco attack the Republic. Barcelona holds out to the end, but falls with little fighting. Hundreds of thousands flee into France. Lluis Companys, president of the Generalitat, is executed with thousands of others in the castle of Montjuïc. Catalan is banned.

The main cathedral's 'Gothic' front completed in the 19th century

1940s– **1950s**	Shunned by the bulk of the international community, Spain starves in the *Noche Negro* ('black night') after the war.
1952	Spain accepts financial aid and allows U.S. bases in the country.
1960s	Two million immigrants, mainly from the south, arrive looking for work and shanty towns are thrown up around the city.
1975	Death of General Franco celebrated with free *cava* in the streets. Catalan is a recognised language again.
1979	Statute of Autonomy gives Catalonia some independence.
1992	Olympic Games held in Barcelona after a massive six-year restructuring and rebuilding programme.
1999	The new National Theatre is completed and the Liceu reopens after rebuilding following a fire.
2004	Forum 2004 sees the city extended north to the River Besòs in a year of cultural activity.

THE CATALAN FLAG

The legend behind the design of the shield and flag of Catalonia is that it was a grant of arms from Charles the Bald, grandson of Charlemagne and King of the West Franks. In 897 he was doing battle with the Moors near Lleida when, in answer to a summons, Guifré el Pelós (Wilfred the Hairy), the first Count of Barcelona, came to his aid. Wilfred's intervention turned the course of the battle, but in his finest hour he was slain. As he lay dying Charles dipped his fingers in the count's blood and dragged it across his golden shield, thus inventing *Les Quatre Barres*, the four bands of the Catalan flag.

The magic fountain and Palau Nacional on Montjuïc

Governance

The city is governed from the heart of the old town in Plaça St Jaume where the flags of Spain, Catalonia and Barcelona fly. The Ajuntament (town hall) is in the Casa de la Ciutat, flanked by statues of local dignitaries and city police (the Guardia Urbana). Facing it across the cobbled square is the Palau de la Generalitat, home of the regional government, guarded by the autonomous police force (the Mossos d'Esquadra) and the figure of the patron saint of Catalonia, St George.

Jordi Pujol, retiring President of Catalonia

Spain is a constitutional monarchy ruled over by King Juan Carlos who has been on the throne since the restoration of the monarchy in 1975. The country is governed from the Cortes (parliament) in the capital, Madrid. The king appoints a prime minister from the party with the majority of seats in the Chamber of Deputies, the lower house, to which 350 members are elected by proportional representation every 4 years. An upper house contains the Senate, with 49 members from each of the 14 autonomous regions of Spain. Catalonia is one of these.

The Generalitat

The autonomous region of Catalonia is governed by the Generalitat in Barcelona. For more than a quarter of a century it has been dominated by the conservative Convergència i Unió party under the charismatic presidency of Jordi Pujol.

The fact that the Generalitat, representing the country as well as the towns, has always been under conservative control, while the Ajuntament, representing the more radical view of the city, has during this time been in socialist hands, leads to inevitable clashes. In 1999 the elected socialist mayor Pasqual Maragall tried to break this mould by challenging Pujol for the Catalan presidency. He was

The Palau de la Generalitat under wraps for restoration work

unsuccessful, and was succeeded in the mayor's office by his deputy, Joan Clos i Matheu, who won a four-year term in 1999.

Council meetings are held in the Saló de Cent, a magnificent Gothic hall built in the golden reign of Pere III (1336–87) for the city's original Council of a Hundred. It is only occasionally open to the public.

The elected members of the Generalitat sit in the Parlament de Catalunya, in a building they share with the Museu d'Art Modern in the Parc de la Ciutadella.

Rights and privileges

The autonomy won from Madrid is relatively new, but for centuries, first under the count-kings of Barcelona and then under civic rulers, Catalonia was an independent nation that governed itself. Its parliament, the Corts Catalanes, was formally established in 1359 to represent the nobility, church and people and to regulate the city's finances and ensure its rights.

These rights, or *usatges*, were of fundamental importance to Catalans, and each time they have been threatened there has been trouble. In trying to shake free from Madrid, Catalonia has sided with France against Spain, to its cost. The last time it declared independence was in 1931 under the Republican leader of the Generalitat, Francesc Macià. It lasted less than a day.

There are Catalans today who want a complete break with Madrid, notably the underground organisation Terra Lliure ('free land'), but autonomy has taken the edge off their demands.

The Catalan Parliament building in Parc de la Ciutadella

Catalan Nationalism

Catalans are clearly sentimental about traditions like the *sardana,* the national dance, banned by Franco and danced clandestinely, or Montserrat, the 'Sawn Mountain', the spiritual centre of Catalonia. But Catalan nationalism, this feeling of a separate identity which crosses all social and political divides, has much deeper roots. A quick look at history shows why. Long before Spain existed as a state, Catalonia was a nation with its own government, laws and institutions, its own bickering feudal lords, semi-legendary dashing warrior rulers with outlandish names, imperial glory days and dynastic ructions.

The government, the Generalitat de Catalunya, existed in the 13th century, and the Barcelona Corts was one of the earliest parliaments in Europe.

In the 8th century, a cluster of counties with a common sense of identity emerged as a buffer state between Charlemagne's Christian empire and Moorish Spain. In 878 Wilfred the Hairy united several counties and proclaimed himself Count of Barcelona, and the embryonic Catalonia soon asserted its independence from the Frankish kings.

When the County of Barcelona was united with the Kingdom of Aragon by marriage in 1137, each people kept its own language, laws and institutions. Catalonia–Aragon – known as the Crown of Aragon – pushed south and east. By the 13th century, Barcelona rivalled Genoa and Venice as a maritime power, ruling over an empire that included Sicily, Sardinia, Naples and Athens.

But with the marriage of Ferdinand II of Aragon to Isabella of Castile, Catalan power began to wane. While Portugal and Holland emerged with independence from the War of the Spanish Succession (1701–13), Catalonia was occupied and severely punished by the victorious Philip V. An entire Barcelona neighbourhood was razed to build a citadel, on the site of what is now the Parc de la Ciutadella. All Catalonia's institutions were abolished, its universities closed, its *modernisme* for which Barcelona is so well known. Catalonia's limited Statute of Autonomy and political voice during the second republic was short-lived, as Spain sank into chaos and finally civil war. With Franco's victory in 1939, Catalonia was punished once again. Resistance simmered underground. Two years after Franco's death, the Generalitat was provisionally restored. On 11 September 1977, one million Catalans staged a massive demonstration to demand the re-establishment of the Statute of Autonomy. This was ratified in October 1979, giving Catalonia a measure of home rule as an 'autonomous community' within the Spanish state.

Today many of Catalonia's aspirations have been achieved, although the industrious Catalans, who contribute the lion's share to the public purse, are ever watchful of the centralising and retrograde forces perceived to emanate from Madrid. In the face of globalisation, Catalonia now promotes itself as a dynamic pluralist society embodying justice, equality and sustainability, an innovative force in the new Europe.

language banned: it became an outlying province of the new centralist Spanish state. Catalonia neither forgave nor forgot. The fall of Barcelona on 11 September 1714 is still solemnly commemorated today.

In the mid-19th century the Catalan economy took off with the industrial revolution, and Catalonia soon became the most enterprising and prosperous region of Spain. The *Renaixença* (Renaissance) movement to restore Catalan culture and language gained momentum. The effervescence of the period is embodied by the fabulous

Left: The Catalan flag flies alongside the Spanish flag
Above: The revival of traditions like 'Castells' has been ardent since Franco's death
(Castellers of Barcelona)

The Gran Teatre del Liceu

Culture

One of the great attractions of Barcelona is that its art, architecture and culture are closely woven into its everyday bustle. A lively cosmopolitan arts scene, exuberant Mediterranean festivals and a notable work ethic combine to give the city a unique flair.

Barcelona is a city of worldwide architectural fascination, with layer upon layer of history built into its urban fabric: the remains of the Roman walls and the soaring Catalan Gothic of the basilica of Santa Maria del Mar, the

Dazzling interior of Domènech i Montaner's Palau de la Música

heady flights of *modernisme* and the far-reaching urban redevelopment of the 1980s and 1990s. As well as the must-see buildings by Gaudí and his contemporaries, a walk around the Eixample offers more private glimpses of *modernista* vestibules and shops. Barcelonans are extremely proud of their cultural heritage, which they feel is part of their identity. Shopkeepers, for example, lovingly conserve and display antique cash registers, sewing machines and ceramic jars.

Another salient example of the cultural texture of Barcelona life is the World Heritage-listed Hospital de la Santa Creu i Sant Pau, which has the distinction of being a fully operational 21st-century teaching hospital. Linking up with the spirit of the *modernista* movement, one of the key ideas underpinning the pre-Olympic urban renewal was the 'monumentalisation' of the outlying neighbourhoods and their promotion as centres of culture: this was the rationale behind sculptures like Claes Oldenburg's giant *Matches* up in the Vall d'Hebron, and, more recently, the building of the Teatre Nacional and the Auditori (and a shopping mall, of course) in a hitherto derelict area close to one of the city's main traffic nexuses.

Museums

Barcelona is also famed for its large number of museums: ethnology, maritime, decorative arts, footwear, automata, geology, perfume... as well as highlights like the Picasso Museum and the world's finest collection of Romanesque art at the Museu Nacional d'Art de Catalunya. In addition to the permanent displays, there is always a wide choice of temporary exhibitions at the Museu Picasso, the Fundació Joan Miró, the Fundació Antoni Tàpies, the MACBA, the Pedrera and the Caixa Fòrum, amongst others.

Theatre and dance

Vibrancy is a word much bandied about when talking about Barcelona, and it is no less applicable to the performing-arts scene. Barcelona has a long tradition of theatre, which is now flourishing, both in the range and quality of productions and in the number of theatre-goers. Many small theatres across the city stage classic works in translation as well as contemporary plays. The Teatre Nacional de Catalunya takes a new look at classical theatre, both national and international, stages the latest in contemporary theatre productions, and hosts multidisciplinary events and dance performances. As its name suggests, the Mercat de les Flors theatre used to be Barcelona's flower market. Dance plays a major part in its stimulating programme which features many international visiting groups. In fact Barcelona has

Sardanes are danced religiously every Sunday in the Cathedral Square

The Camp Nou football stadium – pride of all 'Barça' fans

developed a first-class reputation for innovative contemporary dance, with a number of small and medium-sized companies, such as the Companyia Gelabert-Azzopardi, now enjoying international prestige. First-rate Spanish dance and flamenco companies also regularly visit.

Music
There is a tremendous variety of music to be enjoyed in Barcelona, from classical symphonies to opera, ballet, jazz, flamenco, pop, rock, indie and experimental music. Concerts, recitals and festivals abound. In recent years contemporary and experimental music has been promoted with events such as the Sonar Advanced Music Festival, the BAM (Barcelona Acció Musical) for independent music, the Jazz Festival and the Guitar Festival. The new Auditori, designed by Rafael Moneo and opened in 1999, is now the focal point for the

city's musical events and is home to the Barcelona Symphony Orchestra. In addition, it stages seasons such as Ibercámera with many visiting orchestras and soloists and offers a full programme of all kinds of music including jazz, world music and flamenco. The Orfeo Catalá choir is the flagship survivor of the patriotic and sociocultural movement of the late 19th century, when over 150 choral groups were founded in Catalonia. It gives numerous concerts every year as well as acting as choir to the Barcelona Symphony Orchestra and others. Badly damaged in a fire in 1994, the Liceu opera house has been rebuilt and upgraded and offers a full programme of opera, ballet, concerts and recitals.

Exciting venues
Venues like the fabulous Palau de la Música Catalana are worth seeing whatever is on the bill. And what a

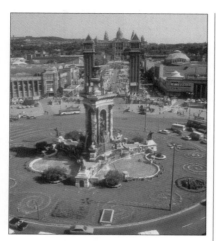

Plaça Espanya below Montjuïc's venues

pleasure it is to glide up into the quiet fragrant pines of Montjuïc on the escalators from Plaça Espanya and see the city spread out below, on one's way to a concert at the Palau Sant Jordi, now an integral part of Barcelona's skyline. Inside it is incredibly light and airy, even when packed to capacity for the likes of Bruce Springsteen, Bon Jovi or Paul McCartney.

Festival del Grec

The culmination of the performing arts calendar is the Festival del Grec (Grec Summer Festival), Barcelona's biggest performing arts festival held in late June and July. This was originally staged at the neo-Greek amphitheatre on Montjuïc, hence the name. The amphitheatre is now joined by other venues around the city, although the Grec itself is delightful on a hot summer's night. One of Europe's biggest arts festivals, the Grec offers national (Castilian and Catalan) and international theatre, dance (mainly contemporary), and music for all tastes, especially Brazilian and flamenco.

WORKING BARCELONA

Barcelonans definitely subscribe to the work ethic – they are hard-working and punctual and greatly prize efficiency – but festivals such as the Festa Major de Gràcia, the Dia de Sant Jordi and the Mercè (see pp22–3) show that they are still a Mediterranean people. They are innovative and traditional at the same time. One unique 'performance' that should not be missed is the dancing of the *sardana*, the intricate national dance of Catalonia, every Sunday at noon in front of the cathedral, accompanied by a traditional band called a *cobla*. It's democratic: if you want to join in, just enter the circle.

The Barcelona Stock Exchange in Passeig de Gràcia

Open-air venue in the summer Grec Festival

Festivals

Barcelonans have a special flair for combining work, fun and creative imagination. The northern-style work ethic is by no means at odds with Mediterranean vibrancy, as the city's exuberant red-letter days show.

Cavalcada dels Reis (Three Kings Parade)
5 January
Fantastically colourful procession on the eve of Epiphany. The Three Kings or Wise Men arrive from the Orient by boat, are welcomed on the quayside (Moll de la Fusta) by the mayor, parade around the city with their retinues hurling tons of sweets into the crowd, then take presents to sleeping children.

Carnestoltes (Carnival)
Late February/early March
The final outburst of pagan indulgence before Lent. City-wide partying and processions, fireworks, dancing in Plaça Catalunya, concerts. It is business as usual in this commercially minded city: the traders in the Boquería and other markets keep on trading – in fancy dress.

Dia de Sant Jordi – Dia del Llibre (Book Day)
23 April
A memorable day for Catalans blending fun and romance, culture and hard-headed business sense. Sant Jordi (St George) is the patron saint of Catalonia, and his feast day, which is also the anniversary of Cervantes' death, is celebrated by exchanging gifts of books and roses. The day, however, is not a public holiday, so the festivities blend in with daily life. Booksellers set up stalls in the streets complete with buckets of red roses (a discount of 10% is given on all books), book launches and author signings are scheduled, and at night the usual partying takes place – dances, discos, fireworks. Benefits are also organised, such as book collections for hospitals.

14 festival de guitarra de barcelona

The Guitar Festival, one of many in Barcelona's calendar

Fira de Sant Ponç
11 May
Feast day of the patron saint of beekeepers and herbalists: stalls selling honey, herbs, candied fruit and other natural products in Carrer Hospital in the heart of the old city. Colourful and very, very fragrant.

L'Ou Com Balla (The Dancing Egg)
Corpus Christi–early June
The Dancing Egg is a very old custom: a previously emptied egg is left to 'dance' on the jets of the fountain in the cathedral cloister and other courtyards in the Gothic Quarter: Casa de l'Ardiaca, Ateneu Barcelonès, Museu Frederic Marès. The fountains are decorated with flowers making it one of the most curious and picturesque traditions in the city's folklore.

Nit de Sant Joan, Nit de Foc (St John's Night)
Night of 23/24 June
The most obviously pagan of all the festivals, marking the summer solstice.

Explosive celebrations on the night of Sant Joan

A wild night of fireworks and partying, although the traditional bonfires have been banned from the city. Impressive formal firework displays, live music, dancing, *cava* flowing on the Rambla. Revellers wind up on the beach at sunrise. Of course, 24th June is a public holiday.

Festa Major de Gràcia (Gràcia Annual Fete)
Mid-August
Vibrant neighbourhood festival (*see pp72–3*) offering non-stop open-air entertainment for all ages and tastes. The Festa kicks off with giants and castle-builders and goes out, literally, with a bang: a massive and spectacular firework display.

La Diada de Catalunya
11 September
Catalonia's National Day (*see pp16–17*). Public holiday. A solemn occasion for political demonstrations and the laying of wreaths on monuments to the fallen, rather than for festive celebrations.

Festes de La Mercè
Week around 24 September
A week-long extravaganza centred around the feast day of Barcelona's patron saint, Our Lady of Mercy. The Mercè has everything – processions, giants, castle-builders, fire dragons, music of all kinds, free-entry days at museums, visual and performing arts shows, craft and food fairs, fireworks and the associated Contemporary Music Festival and Barcelona Alternative Music Festival.

It may well come as a surprise to the visitor to hear Barcelona people speaking a sharp staccato tongue or to see what looks like a jumble of Spanish, French and Italian on street signs and restaurant menus: *entrada* (entrance), *sortida* (exit), *museu* (museum), *ciutat* (city), *església* (church), *pa* (bread), *carn* (meat), *vi* (wine) and so on. This is Catalan, the official language of Catalonia alongside Castilian (Spanish), according to the Spanish Constitution of 1978.

Spoken by over six million people and understood by ten million (in Catalonia, Valencia, the Balearic Islands, Roussillon in southern France, Andorra, and Alghero in Sardinia), Catalan is not a dialect, as is often mistakenly assumed, but a fully-fledged language derived from the Latin spoken in northeastern

Spain during the Roman empire. It is therefore a sister language to Spanish, French, Italian and Portuguese. It boasts a cultural and literary tradition dating from the 12th century, with its own literary Golden Age in the 15th century. In that period trade flourished and Catalan was used as a lingua franca throughout the Mediterranean. It was also honed into a first-rate literary language: Joanot Martorell's novel of chivalry *Tirant lo Blanc*, published in 1490, was read and praised by Cervantes.

But later two attempts were made to wipe out the language. Philip V severely punished Catalonia for fighting against him in the War of the Spanish Succession, and from 1714 abolished all its institutions, closed its universities and banned the language. The late 19th century and early 20th centuries saw a great revival, the Renaixença, which was curtailed by the Spanish Civil War.

Under Franco's repressive regime, Catalan was banned entirely from public use and an entire generation of Catalans grew up unable to read or write their mother tongue. Artists and writers, scientists and scholars flocked into exile. The poignant 1962 novel, *La Plaça del Diamant*, set in Barcelona's Gràcia neighbourhood during the Spanish Civil War, was written by Mercè Rodoreda in exile in Switzerland and has been translated into more languages than any other Catalan work; its title in English is *The Time of the Doves*.

Since the granting of the Statute of Autonomy in 1979, the government of Catalonia has vigorously implemented a policy of 'linguistic normalisation' designed to promote Catalan as an ordinary working language in all walks of life: education, the media, the arts, science and technology, business, public administration, the courts. As a result, Catalan now seems to be in excellent shape, happily co-existing with Castilian. Most Barcelonans are bilingual and slip automatically back and forth between the two languages depending on who they are talking to. Courtesy and consideration rule, and very few are such extreme nationalists that they will refuse to speak Castilian to non-Catalan speakers. Many writers and journalists, actors, singers and TV presenters work in both languages, and the main Spanish language papers publish supplements in Catalan. One popular paper, *El Periódico*, publishes a daily edition in each language. Catalan has two TV channels and numerous radio stations. It has its rock bands, websites and incomprehensible teenage slang, its crime thrillers, poetry and pop psychology best-sellers, its TV chat shows and soap operas.

While non-Catalan speakers claim they are discriminated against on the job market, the Catalans insist that 'positive discrimination' is crucial to prevent degeneration into a local patois. They still fear for the future of their language: the long shadows of Philip V and General Franco still lurk in the Catalan collective unconscious.

Left: The Barcelona Manifesto on Rambla Catalunya
Above: Barcelona's main Catalan newspaper

Impressions

If you drink the waters of the famous Font de Canaletes in La Rambla, legend has it you will fall in love with the city and inevitably return. According to the no less uncertain science of statistics, Barcelona has invariably come out in the top five European cities as a favourite destination, best place to open a business, or for its superior quality of life. Few visitors, whether on a bargain break, romantic escapade or business trip, can resist its charms. Maybe the waters of the fountain are to blame. Whatever it is, Barcelona's undeniable magnetism makes people return.

Foster's communication tower pricks the Collserola hills

When to visit

Such is Barcelona's new popularity that flights and hotels fill with great alacrity, especially over peak periods like Christmas, Easter and European summer holidays. So do La Rambla, the Sagrada Família, the Picasso Museum and other key tourist sights. The beaches are crammed with locals at weekends from mid-June to mid-September. So if you have the choice of travelling out of season it is recommended: there are fewer crowds and the flights are correspondingly cheaper. Besides, Barcelona is a city for exploring on foot, observing street-life and architecture, visiting museums and savouring long lunches – all of which are better without blistering heat. The ideal time is spring or autumn, though as perfect weather can never be guaranteed you could be equally lucky in the middle of December, often characterised by crisp sunny days.

The city lies densely between the Collserola hills and the Mediterranean

Areas of the city

Getting a grip on the basic layout of Barcelona and deciding which parts you want to visit is easy. Looking at a city map you can see how it lies between the Collserola range and the sea, enclosed by the hill of Montjuïc and the River Besòs. The identifiable labyrinth of narrow streets between Plaça Catalunya and the

The vast industrial port spreads out beneath the hill of Montjuïc

port is the Ciutat Vella (the 'old town') which includes the Gothic quarter.

The contrastingly geometrical grid of streets which spreads between the Ciutat Vella and the former villages of Sants, Sarrià, Gràcia and Horta is the Eixample, built according to Ildefons Cerdà's extension plan in the mid-19th century. The heart of the Eixample contains some of the finest *modernista* buildings. This was like a new town, built to cope with the expanding population bursting out of the old city walls.

Climbing up the hills are either smart residential districts or (further away from the centre) denser, humbler residential areas where cheap housing was thrown up to cope with the influx of immigrants from other parts of Spain in the 1950s and 1960s. The waterfront comprises the huge industrial port, the new marinas and 4km of beaches stretching to the River Besòs, where a neglected wasteland is now being

developed as the site for the Forum 2004 (*see pp58–9*). Just behind the beaches are the districts of Barceloneta, Vila Olímpica, Poble Nou (a 19th-century industrial area part of which was razed to build the Olympic Village in 1992), and the newest residential zone of the city, Diagonal Mar.

Beyond Barcelona

For anyone here for longer than a week the city is happily easy to get out of. The suburbs just behind the Collserola range are readily accessible by local trains managed by the Generalitat (FGC), as is the hilltop village of Vallvidrera and the surrounding woods. RENFE, the national train service, has local and regional trains serving the coastal strip north and south and beyond to the Pyrenees.

Public transport (or motorbike ...) is the best way to get around Barcelona

A walk down La Rambla is a good starting point

Where to begin
It is nearly all worth exploring, but do not attempt to do everything on a first visit. One of the joys of Barcelona is to wander around observing small details, corner shops, a market-stall, a Romanesque arch, a human statue, the speedy Catalans, or to linger in a medieval patio listening to the trickle of a fountain, or at a pavement café watching the colourful world go by. Absorb the real atmosphere of this Mediterranean city by just being in its midst.

To get an overall picture of the place without risking total exhaustion the official tourist bus is a good option (*see Practical Guide, pp180, 189*). Its two routes cover the key spots, so you can leap off when something interests you, or identify places you want to return to. Alternatively, get a bird's eye view from the cable car across the port on a clear day: identify the layout of the city while enjoying the peace of the ride and keeping the kids happy.

How to get around
Barcelona is manageable on foot, though a combination of walking and the excellent public transport system is best. Avoid driving at all costs unless you are aiming to keep stress levels high. Local drivers are in a hurry and know

where they are going, so they have little patience for outsiders trying to cut across five lanes of traffic while looking at maps. Besides, parking is problematic. The metro (underground), bus and city trains (FGC) are efficient, with an economic system that enables you to transfer from one to another (within a reasonable space of time) on the same ticket, the multiple card T10 usable by more than one person. When all else fails the distinctive black and yellow taxis are usually at hand, and reasonably priced.

Do as the locals...
It is a personal choice, but fitting in as far as possible with the local customs and way of life can make for a more enriching visit. It does not mean generously bestowing kisses on every stranger you meet, nor a crash course in the language – but to avoid standing out as the vulnerable tourist, and becoming frustrated, try to be aware of the differences.

The Catalans are cool dressers, experts at the casual smart. They manage to wear just the right kit for the beach, but strictly for the beach, not for restaurants or church visits. When the sun shines in the winter months they may wear a lighter jacket, but never a sleeveless t-shirt. An effort to communicate in either Catalan or Spanish is well received, even if it never gets beyond *bon dia*.

Do not expect to rush round in the midday heat, shopping or sightseeing. Many shops and businesses close, even in the winter, as lunch is all-important. By eating at the same time as the locals you get a better deal: the *menu del dia* is an economic set menu offered by all restaurants, but only at lunchtimes. A short rest after the large meal will recharge the batteries so you can make the most of the late closing of shops and museums, and is essential if you want to cope with the nightlife that only gets into its stride after midnight.

You can always fall into a taxi when exhaustion sets in

Barcelona

Most of the places a visitor wants to see – and certainly more than can be conquered in a single visit – are within striking distance of Plaça Catalunya, hub of the city, which marks the divide between the old town and the new.

The large open square of Plaça Catalunya is a gathering and meeting place. Underground is a metro and main railway station, as well as a tourist office, and beside it is the city's best known department store, El Corte Inglés.

Detail of the spire on Gaudí's Palau Güell

Seawards from here (inconveniently, Barcelona refuses to sit on any map facing north) is La Rambla, one of the great thoroughfares of the world, which should be the first street to roam, heading down to the imposing statue of Christopher Columbus and the port, where there is always something to see.

The old town...

The old town lies either side of La Rambla. The most ancient part, the Barri Gòtic, is around the cathedral and royal palace, and nothing is more gratifying than becoming completely lost in its myriad streets. On the far side of Via Laietana were the homes of the medieval nobility, such as those in Carrer Montcada, where the Museu Picasso is located. The waterfront here contains the fishing community of Barceloneta and, beyond it, the pleasure beaches and restaurant-filled Olympic Port.

On the other side of La Rambla is El Raval, the traditional working district of the city, with the startlingly modern Museu d'Art Contemporani de Barcelona (MACBA). Beyond El Raval the hill of Montjuïc rises up to the castle, passing en route a couple of other

A tiny decorative part of the huge Nativity façade of the Sagrada Família

great art institutions, the Museu Nacional d'Art de Catalunya (MNAC) and the Fundació Miró, both of which are well worth seeking out.

...and the new
The Plaça Catalunya marks the start of the Eixample, the 19th-century expansion, and this is where the *modernista* architecture lies, with Gaudí's Park Güell some distance behind his unmissable Sagrada Família. This is also where you will find designer Barcelona. Start putting on the style in the Rambla de Catalunya and Passeig de Gràcia, two of the city's most elegant streets.

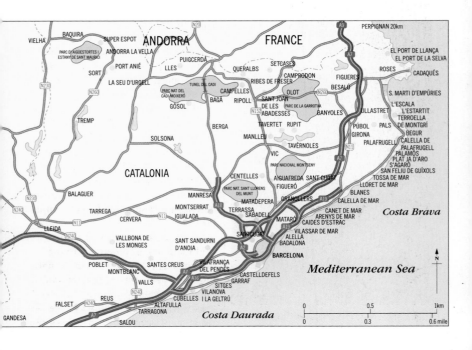

Barceloneta and the Beaches

Alphabetically, the sites of Barcelona begin with Barceloneta and the beaches that stretch north from the port towards the River Besòs. Until the development of the 1992 Olympic Games, this was the city's industrial heartland where goods trucks shunted along the shore. Now it has been reclaimed for the city's leisure and pleasure and is a particularly popular place for eating out.

Traditional lanteen-sail boats

Barceloneta, 'little Barcelona', has a flavour all of its own. This is traditionally the fishermen's district of Barcelona. Not much fishing goes on in Barceloneta's port these days, but there are still a score of boats in the fishing port by Torre de Rellotge, the former harbour lighthouse. Nearby is the Torre St Sebastià, the cable car stop that connects to the World Trade Center in the main port and goes on up to Montjuïc. Cars leave every 15 minutes.

Displaced residents

Barceloneta was built on a grid system in a triangle of land between the Marina Port Vell and the sea to house more than a thousand people displaced from the maritime district of La Ribera – then 'the happiest quarter of Barcelona', according to the 19th-century poet Jacinct Verdaguer. In 1718, following Barcelona's defeat by the Bourbon Felipe V, the quarter had been brutally pulled down, with no compensation, to build La Ciutadella (*see pp102–3*). In fact the displaced had to wait more than a generation before the one-storey buildings went up to re-house them. Its fifteen streets, crossed by five avenues, faced the citadel, keeping them in a line of fire so that any disturbance could easily be controlled. In the 19th century the one-storey houses gained upper floors, but there is still a harmony in these streets of small houses and breezy washing lines.

The Olympic port with Gehry's 'Fish'

Seaside restaurants

A more recent act of brutality was the destruction of the *chiringuitos*, the shacks on the shore where afternoons could be whiled away eating fabulous seafood with your toes in the sand. But such vandalism may be forgiven when eating at the new crop of restaurants, many of them run by the former *chiringuito* owners, such as Can Majó in Almirall Aixada 23 (*tel: 932 21 54 55*).

The restaurants that line the Avinguda Joan de Borbó on the port side of Barceloneta have long been popular, inexpensive places to eat seafood, but it is the new ones around the Port Olímpic, at the centre of the beaches, that have grabbed the attention of Barcelonans, who make their way here for both lunch and dinner.

Socialist utopia

In fact Barcelonans have wholeheartedly embraced the new seafront. The former industrial area, Nova Icaria, named after a 19th-century socialist utopia, has been transformed and the former industrial buildings of Poble Nou have been snapped up as art studios and workshops. And as the whole axis of the city drifts north, attention is centred on Forum 2004 and the Diagonal Mar (*see pp58–9*).

ICARIA

Poble Nou is the former Nova Icaria, which took its name from a book by a French idealist, Étienne Cabet. Born in Dijon, Cabet went to England where he was influenced by Robert Owen and where, like Karl Marx 50 years later, he researched in the British Library. The result was *A Voyage to Icaria*, published in 1839, about a Utopian socialist society. Eight years later, a group of Icarians in Barcelona started up a journal with the slogan *Vamos a Icaria!* And that is what they did: with Cabet, a number of them set sail for America to found a new community of brotherly love. It was a disaster and Cabet died in Illinois, but the name of Icaria was given to the new industrial quarter of Barcelona.

Designer bars and restaurants line the shore

Walk: Barceloneta and the Beaches

Barcelona's beaches stretch 4.2km (3 miles) from the fishing quarter of Barceloneta to the new developments at Parc Diagonal Mar and the River Besòs. They are more crowded nearer Barceloneta and around the Port Olímpic, which is thick with restaurants and bristling with masts. This is the place to get your roller skates on, to walk the dog, or to go for a morning swim or jog.

Allow a couple of hours.

Begin at Barceloneta metro (line 4, or buses 14 and 59 from La Rambla). Return on the metro at Poble Nou (line 4).

1 Plaça de la Barceloneta

Step one block on from the Passeig Joan de Borbó beside Port Vell to find this tranquil square at the heart of the fishermen's quarter. With café tables and shady trees, it is overlooked by Sant Miquel del Port, which, like the rest of the district, was built by a military engineer, Pedro Cermeño. This explains its Baroque appearance – a style otherwise absent from the city. A few steps away is the Plaça del Font where the covered market operates from 7am to 3pm every day. The flower-covered restaurant beside it, one of many popular restaurants in Barceloneta, is the oldest in the district, dating from 1763.

2 Platja Sant Sebastià and Platja de la Barceloneta

Between Barceloneta and the Olympic Port, these two beaches are closest to the city and therefore the most popular. Extending 2.2km (1¼ miles), they have all facilities, with an information point, WCs and showers. The favourite time to swim for Barcelonans is the late afternoon, when the sand and sea are saturated with the heat of the sun that is ebbing from the day.

3 Vila Olímpica
(*see pp124–5*)

4 Port Olímpic
The Olympic Port is a place to watch the world sail by, from expensive yachts to capsizing beginners. It has two tiers of restaurants to choose from and at the weekend craft stalls are laid out to catch the roaring trade. An emblem of the port is the huge woven copper fish (*Pez y Esfera*) by Frank Gehry, architect of the Bilbao Guggenheim and the replacement for New York's twin towers, who was nicknamed 'fish' as a child. Gehry also figured out the 14,000sq m (150,000sq ft) of retail, commercial and maritime elements in the 45-storey, 5-star Hotel Arts, which was designed by Bruce Graham. The hotel has 600 rooms, 33 luxury apartments and the Barcelona Casino. Its twin, the MAPFRE building, is devoted to offices.

The *chiringuitos* live, in a different form

5 Parc del Litoral
This green space between the houses and the beach stands as a memento to the Olympics. Two metal sails bear an inscription to mark the opening of the new area in November 1992. La Font del Cobi has a statue of the Olympic mascot designed by Xavier Mariscal, who had one of the pioneering studios in Poble Nou. In the Plaça dels Campions are the names of the 257 gold medallists from the Olympics as well as the handprints of sporting heroes, including the

footballer Pelè, the cyclist Eddie Merckx and the chess player Garry Kasparov. Beside the park are three enormous street lights 23m (75ft) tall, designed by Antoni Rosselló.

6 Platja Nova Mar Bella

Twenty minutes' walk from the port across tons of imported sand, the 640m (700 yard) beach is overlooked by La Oca Mar, a restaurant in the shape of a ship with a terrace on its bow (*tel: 932 25 01 00*).

7 Rambla de Poble Nou

This is the heart of the industrial area and there are a number of interesting former factories in the surrounding streets. There is a small-town feel to the Rambla, with a local casino and social centre halfway up. Opposite is Tio Ché (*No 44*), a handsome ice cream parlour and *orxateria*. On the right of the Rambla as you head inland is Placete de Prim, the oldest part of Poble Nou where a plaque commemorates the idealistic 19th-century socialist Icarians (*see p33*) who lived here. The local market is held nearby in the Plaça Unió.

8 Diagonal Mar

(*see pp56–9*)

All Barcelona heads for the beach; in summer early morning or late afternoon are best

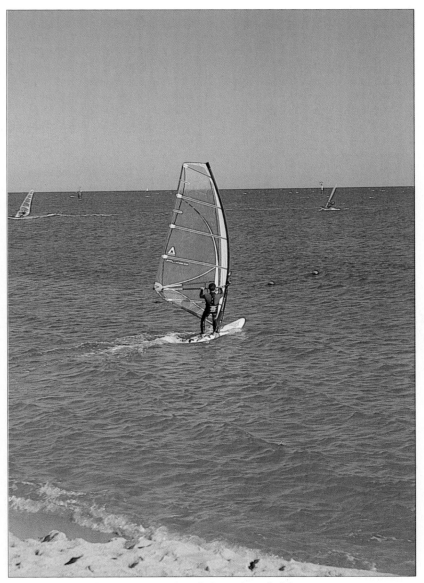

Watersports in the safe Mediterranean, where the breeze is usually light

Good eating is one of the signal features of the Catalan way of life, and Catalan cuisine ranks as the best in Spain alongside the Basque, with a new generation of artistic chefs constantly dreaming up new creations. Eminently Mediterranean and based on nuts, garlic, olive oil, tomatoes, herbs and dried fruit, it reflects the diverse history of the nation, with the influences of different peoples and the varied geography of sea, plains and mountains.

The Catalans work wonders with vegetables. Sautéed with garlic, raisins and pine nuts, the much-maligned spinach is transformed into the tasty and healthy *espinacs a la catalana*, while broad beans are stewed with wine and herbs and grill-sizzled with bacon and

black pudding to become *faves a la catalana*. Salads are quintessential: crisp, light and refreshing, or almost a meal in themselves like *xató* from Sitges, which contains tuna, salt cod and anchovies and is served with piquant *romesco* sauce. Meat, chicken or rabbit *a la plantxa* (on the griddle), with *picada d'all i julivert* (finely chopped garlic and parsley) or *a la brasa* (cooked over a charcoal fire) are timelessly popular. Extra zest is provided by the garlic sauce *allioli*, or by *escalibada*, a salad of grilled and peeled aubergines and peppers. *Botifarra* is the Catalan sausage par excellence, popularly eaten with *mongetes* (haricot beans).

Mar i muntanya is the name of a style that blends the natural products of sea and mountain in such dishes as meat balls with cuttlefish or chicken with prawns. Another staple of the Catalan diet is *bacallà* (salt cod) which is served in innumerable incarnations: as *esqueixada*, for example (shredded raw into a salad of onions, peppers and olives) or *a la llauna* (fried then baked with tomato, red pepper, garlic and parsley).

Seafood and rice dishes abound, too. Why not try *arros negre* ('black rice' – a tasty paella made with squid and their ink) or *fideuà* (noodles cooked in fish stock)? *Suquet de peix* (fish stew) and *calamars farcits* (stuffed squid) are just two of the numerous fish dishes worth sampling. Certain pasta dishes have become naturalised, such as *canalons*, traditionally eaten on 26 December. Mixing apparently unlikely flavours is also typical – for example squid with chocolate, or goose with pears.

Fresh fruit is always a good option for dessert, although for the sweet-toothed, *crema catalana* (a cinnamon- and lemon-flavoured custard with a burnt sugar top) is a must. *Mel i mato* (goat's cheese with honey) and *postre de músic* (mixed nuts and dried fruits) are other traditional desserts.

Catalunya also has a great pastry tradition, with a typical cake made for each and every feast day. *Panellets*, for example, are tiny marzipan cakes made for All Saints, and *coca* is a long flat pastry studded with crystallised fruits and dusted with pine nuts served at summer festivals. At Easter time, the pastissiers vie with each other to create the most elaborate chocolate sculptures.

The most famous exponent of new Catalan cuisine is Ferran Adrià, considered by some to be the best chef in the world. El Bullí, his Costa Brava culinary shrine, won its third Michelin star in 1997, one of only three restaurants in Spain with this ranking. Adrià's cooking is based on the use of fresh ingredients and gives a new twist to classic Mediterranean preparations. His philosophy of providing unexpected contrasts of flavour, temperature and texture inspires the menu of many a restaurant in Barcelona today.

Opposite: Pork products figure largely in Catalan dishes
Above: The healthy accompaniment to tapas – *pa amb tomàquet* – tomatoes rubbed across fresh crusty bread with a trickle of virgin olive oil

Ciutat Vella

The Old Town is the city's heart. Stretching back from the port, it encompasses the Barri Gòtic or Gothic quarter, with the cathedral and royal palace, and the Ribera district where wealthy merchants built mansions such as the ones housing the Picasso Museum. On the other side of La Rambla is El Raval, the working-class district where the city's workshops were built, and where the infamous Barri Xino (Chinese quarter) became a byword for sleaze.

Stained glass window, Santa Maria del Mar

Barri Gòtic

The Gothic quarter is on the site of the Roman settlement, contained within 4th-century walls, a few yards of which remain. Its excavated foundations have been exposed beneath the Royal Palace and a few pillars of a temple to Augustus can be glimpsed inside the doorway of Carrer de Paradis 10. Otherwise there is little of Roman Barcino to be seen.

The royal chapel is built into this section of what was the original Roman wall

A sensible starting point for contemplating the Barri Gòtic is the Plaça Nova outside the cathedral and the **Portal del Bisbe**, one of the original gates leading into the old city, dating from the 1st century. This is the ecclesiastic end of town, with the **Palau Episcopal** and **Casa Ardiaca** (Archdeacon's House), where you can step into a cool courtyard, and note the delightful letterbox carved with swallows and tortoises.

You may not catch the Sunday midday *sardana* dancing in the Pla de la Seu in front of the **cathedral** (or the Thursday antiques and bric-a-brac market) but nobody visiting the cathedral should miss the cloisters, a cool spot with a pretty fountain that can be entered directly on the south side of the cathedral, in Carrer del Bisbe. The geese that rule the roost here may be a legacy of Roman times.

The Avinguda de Catedral continues to Via Laietana, where another chunk of Roman wall runs round the edge of the **Palau Reial Major**, the royal palace. Here the Plaça del Rei is a harmonious corner of the old city, with the wonderful Catalan Gothic portal of the **Palau del Lloctinent**, former home of the Spanish viceroy. But for 500 years the royal palace was the fief of the Barcelona count-kings who reigned in an unbroken line until Martí the Humanist, who gave his name to the arcaded tower in the corner which rises above the magnificent Gothic hall of the palace, the **Saló de Tinell**. It was here that Ferdinand and Isabella, the Catholic monarchs, are said to have received Columbus on his return from the Americas.

Near the **Museu d'Història de la Ciutat** in the corner of the square is the Plaça St Jaume, site of the Roman forum where the **Casa de la Ciutat** (town hall) faces the **Palau de la Generalitat**. The narrow streets around here, built with huge cut stones and impressive doorways, seem hardly to have changed since the Middle Ages. On the Rambla side of the square is **El Call**, the old Jewish quarter. There were three synagogues in this small area and a 14th-century Hebrew tablet remains in Carrer de Marlet 1.

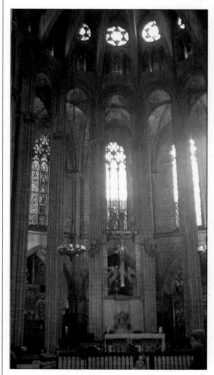

Santa Maria del Mar, the city's finest church

Between here and the Rambla is the **Plaça Sant Josep Oriol**, a lively small square to stop for a drink. Plaça del Pi, which adjoins it, leads to **Carrer Petritxol**, a street of art dealers. Antique shops abound around here, but everywhere in the Barri Gòtic are delightful old shops for browsing.

The Picasso Museum in the Gothic Carrer de Montcada

El Raval

El Raval lies to the left-hand side of La Rambla as you look up from the port. It is traditionally the working-class area of the city, but its regeneration has been going on for some time, most recently with the pulling down of whole blocks to make way for a new Rambla, letting in air and light. The most spectacular innovation, however, was the **Museu d'Art Contemporani de Barcelona** (MACBA), a great slab of white designed by the American architect Richard Meier and dumped down alongside the **Casa de Caritat** (CCCB), the 18th-century house of charity, itself ingeniously turned into a cultural and exhibition space.

Charity for the workers and others was provided by the former city hospital, a series of buildings off the **Carrer Hospital**. Libraries take up most of their space now, but the grounds are pleasant to walk through. Carrer Hospital has an intriguing collection of old shops, selling leather, perfume and miracle cures.

The **Barri Xino**, on the waterfront side of El Raval, is not the rough area it was but some things changed. At the **Bar Pastis** (Carrer Santa Mónica 4) Edith Piaf has not left the turntable since 1947 and at the **Marsella** (Carrer Sant Pau 65) absinthe is still served.

Unexpectedly, there is a major Gaudí building in Carrer Nou de la Rambla. **Palau Güell** is the town house of the architect's patron Eusebi Güell. It is a dark, Gothic place. More cheerful is **Sant Pere de Camp**, St Peter in the Fields, at the far end of Carrer de Sant Pau. This is the only Romanesque church in the city, with some Visigothic traces. Plainsong still fills the small cloister each day.

La Ribera

This area lies on the far side of the Via Laietana and it grew to prosperity during the first major expansion of the city, from the 12th to the 14th centuries. A market and jousting field were sited in El Born, and the merchants built their mansions and palaces close to the activity and business of the port, together with a fine Gothic stock exchange (**La Llotja**) and a magnificent church, **Santa Maria del Mar.**

The best place to feel a sense of this expanding late-medieval city is in the grand Gothic mansions of Carrer de Montcada, where the **Museu Picasso** is just one of several museum and

galleries to take advantage of the buildings' graceful space. Among others are the textile museum (**Museu Tèxtil i d'Indumentària**) and the adjoining **Museu Barbier-Mueller d'Art Precolombi**, with early Latin-American artefacts, and the art galleries of **Sala Montcada** and the **Galeria Maeght**. At the end of the street is the rewarding **El Xampanyet**, a delightful small bar that serves *cava*, Spain's sparkling wine.

The **Mercat del Born** was an open-air market until 1876 when it was covered over with what was then the largest iron structure in Spain, covering 17,200sq m (185,000sq ft). Recent excavations have revealed important pre-18th century foundations. Today the area around the market is a lively nocturnal haunt, with trendy small restaurants and bars.

Palau Güell's wonderfully unique interior

Walk: Ciutat Vella

This walk takes in the most important sites in the old town. It is easy to become side-tracked in the lanes and alleys that meander between the great buildings but do not worry if you get lost – that is half the fun. And you will soon find a landmark to get your bearings.

Allow half a day.

Start at Urquinaona metro (line 1). Jaume I (line 4) in Via Laietana is the nearest Metro at the end of the walk.

1 Palau de la Música Catalana

There are few examples of *modernisme* in the old town and few greater *modernista* buildings than the city music hall, which is a UNESCO World Heritage Site. Designed by Lluís Domènech i Montaner and completed in 1908, it has a dazzling façade of mosaics, statues and brickwork hard to

The sumptuous Palau de la Música Catalana

appreciate in the confines of the street that it fronts. A concert here should not be missed. A beautiful inverted dome of coloured glass diffuses the light in the auditorium, which has sculptures of Richard Wagner and Josep Anselm Clavé, who founded the Orfeó Català choral society for which the building was created.

Carrer de Sant Francesc de Paula 2. Tel: 932 95 72 00. Guided tours (50 min) every 30 min daily 10am–3pm. Admission charge.

2 Catedral

On the site of a Roman temple, the cathedral was begun in 1298 and not completed until the 20th century. Its oldest part is a small Romanesque chapel dedicated to Santa Lucia, though the cathedral is dedicated to Santa Eulàlia, a 4th-century martyr and the city's patron who is entombed in the crypt. The church has a nave and 28 side chapels, with a notable painting by Bernat Martorell (1452) in the Capella Sant Bernat. A large plaque just to the left of the door commemorates the

baptism here of Carib Indians brought back by Columbus in 1493. The cloisters are beautifully cool and keep contented geese.
Plaça de la Seu. Tel: 93 310 71 95. Open daily. Free.

3 Museu Frederic Marès

The most eclectic museum in the city was put together by the sculptor Frederic Marès (1893–1991) in part of the old Royal Palace. Religious art in the basement includes intact portals and a large collection of sculptures from

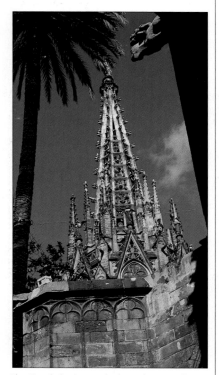

The Catedral spire watched over by gargoyles

around Catalonia. On the three floors above, the collection becomes more whimsical, with pipes, clocks, umbrellas and pin-up postcards.
Plaça de Sant Iu 5–6. Tel: 93 310 58 00. Open: Tue–Sat 10am–7pm, Sun & holidays 10am–3pm. Closed: Mon. Admission charge.

4 Plaça Sant Jaume

The site of the Roman Forum remains the debating centre of the city. The **Casa de la Ciutat** (town hall) dates from the 14th century and its entrance is watched over by Jaume I, who granted Barcelona the right to elect its representatives, and Joan Fiveller, a fiscal hero. Its main chamber is the Saló de Cent, where the city's 100 councillors met. The Saló de les Cròniques on the first floor was decorated in 1929 by Josep-Maria Sert with murals of scenes from Catalan history.

The **Palau de la Generalitat** on the opposite side of the square is guarded by St George, patron saint of Catalonia. Seat of the Generalitat (Catalan government) since the 15th century, it has some fine interior rooms and a beautiful first-floor open patio, the Patí dels Trongers.
Both buildings are open only on special occasions.

5 Palau Reial Major

The royal palace of the count-kings of Barcelona is overlooked by the arcaded Torre de Martí. Beside it is the **Saló del Tinel**, a huge Gothic hall that was the bustling centre of the royal domain. Stairs up the tower begin in the **Capella de Santa Agata**, the royal chapel built against

the Roman wall with a bell tower acting as a watchtower. The altarpiece by Jaume Huguet (1466) is the only remaining decoration in the entire royal complex. Beneath the palace you can see part of the Roman city, which connects underground with the **Museu d'Historia del la Ciutat** on the opposite side of the Plaça del Rei.
Plaça del Rei. Tel: 93 315 11 11. Open: Tue–Sat 10am–8pm, Sun & holidays 10am–2pm.

6 Museu Picasso

The Picasso Museum is housed in three Gothic palaces named after the families who had them built – Berenguer d'Aguilar, Baró de Constallet and Meca – in a street so narrow the roofs nearly touch. The buildings alone are worth a visit; the paintings and drawings by the city's favourite adopted son (*see pp48–9*) make it unmissable.
Carrer Montcada 15–23. Tel: 93 319 63 10. Open: Tue–Sat 10am–8pm, Sun 10am–3pm. Closed: Mon. Admission charge.

7 Església de Santa Maria del Mar

The city's finest church is a simple Gothic masterpiece raised from nothing in 1384 after just 55 years in the building. Its three lofty naves are almost identical and their octagonal columns an impressive 13m (43ft) apart. The 14th-century rose window replaced the original lost in an earth tremor. The acoustics are excellent and there are often concerts here, including jazz.
Carrer Montcada 1. Open daily: 9.30am–1.30pm, 4.30–8pm. Free.

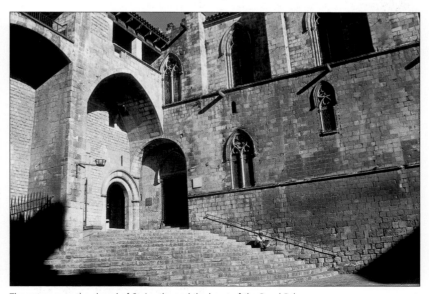

The entrance to the chapel of St Agatha and the heart of the Royal Palace

The Museu Picasso in Barcelona has the largest collection of the artist's works in the world. Much of it is fascinating material from his childhood and precocious art-school years. Though he lived in the city for only a short time, it left an indelible mark on him and his work, and the museum is as much his homage to the city as it is the city's to its talented son.

Pablo Picasso was born in 1881 in Málaga, where his mother, Maria Picasso, came from. His father, José Ruiz Blasco, was an art teacher from the Basque country and he was offered a job teaching in Barcelona's art school, then situated above the Llotja (stock exchange) when Pablo was nearly 14. The family eventually settled in Carrer de Mercè 3 not far from the school, which Pablo began to attend. His precocious talent flourished, and he was a highly accomplished formal painter even in his mid teens.

At the school he made a lifetime friend in the artist Manuel Pallarès, who came from the town of Horta de Ebro. Picasso's subsequent trips to this village are recorded in pictures in the gallery. Fond of the low-life, the two friends visited the prostitutes in Carrer d'Avinyó and their experience inspired *Les Demoiselles d'Avignon* (1906–7, Museum of Modern Art, New York), the painting considered by many historians to be the starting point of modern art.

Picasso's father rented him a studio in Calle de la Plata, 4, where he executed

Contemporary Art Collection

returned sporadically, mostly to see his family, but in 1917 he did a series of paintings in the city when he visited with Diaghilev's Ballet Russe, for which he had painted the scenery.

His feelings about the Civil War were expressed in *Guernica* (Museo Reina Sofia, Madrid), his painting depicting the suffering of the people of the Basque village when it was bombed by Franco's German allies on 26 April 1937, a market day.

The Franco regime kept him in exile but it did not keep his paintings away, and from the mid 1950s the Gaspard Gallery regularly exhibited his work. On these occasions Sabartés would return to Barcelona and it was very much his influence, together with donations of Picassos from his own collection, that led the municipality to establish a museum for his friend in 1963. When Sabartés died five years later, Picasso added to the museum by donating in his memory the 58-picture series *Las Meninas*, a homage to Spain's great painter Diego Velásquez.

In 1970, three years before his death in France, Picasso made further donations of 900 paintings, drawings and other items that had been in his parents' house when he went to live in Paris.

the large canvas of a woman on her sick bed titled *Science and Charity* (197 × 249.5cm), which was sent to the General Fine Arts Exhibition in Madrid in 1897.

Setting up on his own in various studios, Picasso was a regular visitor to Els Quatre Gats, the artists' café in Carrer Montesió, where he had his first exhibition at the age of 20. In this milieu he mingled with the best of Barcelona's contemporary painters, such as Ramon Casas and Santiago Rusiñol, as well as Jaime Sabartés y Gual, a poet and writer the same age as himself, who became a good friend in Paris.

Paris was the place for artists to head for, and in 1904 Picasso set off for the city, leaving Barcelona for good. He

Opposite: Els Quatre Gats café in Carrer Montesió where Picasso had his first exhibition
Above: There is no escaping Picasso!

Walk: Raval

From old buildings that formerly housed thousands of orphans to dazzling modern cultural centres, from avant-garde galleries to trendy bars, this walk in the once-neglected Raval district of the Old Town is a fine example of the fascinating diversity that characterises Barcelona. *Allow 1–2 hours.*

From the top of La Rambla turn into Carrer Bonsuccés which leads into Plaça Bonsuccés. Cut through the arch into Plaça Vicenç Martorell. Some of this walk can be traced on the map of La Rambla (p87).

Begin with coffee in Plaça Catalunya

Casa de la Misericòrdia
Now used as municipal offices for the Ciutat Vella district, this building dates from 1583. It was one of many religious institutions and convents that were situated on this side of La Rambla, just outside the city wall. A testimony to its past as a hospice for abandoned children is a curious hole in the wall, through which babies were passed to merciful nuns.

La Central del Raval
Cut through the café of the adjoining bookshop which is in the chapel of the Casa de la Misericòrdia to get an idea of the extent of this medieval complex, and to see Barcelona 20th-century design at its best – a clever combination of ancient and modern.
Pass the books to the entrance in the street Elisabets, then right into Elisabets and right again into Montalegre.

Centre de Cultura Contemporània de Barcelona
Known as the CCCB, this centre for contemporary culture has a busy programme of exhibitions and diverse cultural activities. A former orphanage, it was converted into this magnificent space by architects Piñon and Vilaplana, part of the flurry of activity pre- and post-Olympics.

Museu d'Art Contemporani (MACBA)
The enormous building that houses the Contemporary Art Museum sits large and dazzling on the Plaça dels Angels. Its collection includes post-1950s Catalan and Spanish art, as well as some international pieces, and interesting temporary exhibitions (*see p135*).
From Plaça dels Angels go down Carrer dels Angels and turn left into Carrer del Carme (see p87).

Antic Hospital de la Santa Creu
Often overlooked, this gothic complex is a gem. It was used as a hospital until the 1920s, when it moved to the new Santa Creu i Sant Pau designed by *modernista* Domènech i Montaner in the Eixample (*see p116*). The Institut d'Estudis

Catalans with its magnificent tile work now occupies the convalescent wing. Wander through the shady courtyard perfumed by orange blossom, past the Library of Catalonia and the Massana art school until you emerge in Carrer Hospital.

Turn right into Carrer Hospital and follow it until it opens into the Rambla del Raval.

Rambla del Raval

This new Rambla is emblematic of the city council's policy of urban regeneration. Despite fierce criticism they went ahead and bulldozed several streets of old but occupied housing to create this bright boulevard. Bathed in bright sunlight, it contrasts sharply with the dark, putrid streets of the past where people skulked in doorways.

Today local residents seem to enjoy it as a leisure space, sitting at its terrace cafés while kids speed by on bikes and skateboards.

The rotund cat at the end of the Rambla is unmistakably the work of Colombian artist Botero.

The dazzling MACBA, Museum of Contemporary Art

Barcelona's fortune was founded on the sea. Once a great naval power, it had a dockyard that furnished the royal fleet and rivalled those of Genoa and Venice. From here Catalans set off on their conquests of the Balearics and places further afield, and it was here that Christopher Columbus stepped ashore in triumph after his discovery of America.

Barcelona's mastery of the seas began in the reign of Jaume I, el Conqueridor (James I, 1213–76). He extended

Catalonia's territories, taking the Balearic islands of Mallorca and Ibiza from the Moors. During his reign the *Llibre de Consulat de Mar* was drawn up as a code of trading practice throughout the Mediterranean.

Catalonia had a flamboyant admiral in Roger de Llúria, scourge of the French, who killed the Provençal admiral Guíllen Corner in single combat when he jumped aboard the French ship in an encounter off Malta in 1283. More menacing was Roger de Flor, described by a contemporary as 'of terrible aspect, quick in gesture and imperious in action'. He was admiral of the fleet of King Frederick of Sicily during a French attempt to recapture the island, and he went on to command a fearful crew of Catalan and Aragonese mercenaries known as the Almogàvars.

By this time Barcelona was the wealthiest mercantile state in the Mediterranean, importing gold from north Africa and spices from the east. A century before Columbus set sail from Seville, the great Catalan poet Ramon Lull (1232–1315) wrote *Arte de Navigar*, in which he detailed methods of navigation using charts and astrolabes and making the first mention of the magnetic needle. Realising the earth was round, he foresaw the Americas – 'a continent against which the water strikes when displaced, as happens on our side, which is, in respect to the other, the eastern side'.

When Columbus returned from his second voyage in 1494, he was greeted in Barcelona by Ferdinand and Isabella. But the discovery of the New World held few benefits for Barcelona, as trade was granted exclusively to Seville and the Atlantic port of Cadiz.

By the 16th century the seas were largely at the mercy of Barbary pirates and corsairs. The northern Mediterranean states were finally galvanised into action, and trees were felled across Catalonia to build the ships that sailed from its shores to join the Venetian forces against the Ottomans. They met off the Greek coast at Lepanto, led by the flagship of Don John of Austria, which now resides in replica in Barcelona's former dockyards, the Drassanes.

Mercantile fortunes did not revive until the 19th century when Barcelona was permitted to trade with South America. Many Catalans had gone to make their fortunes in Cuba, and Habaneras, sea shanties from Havana, are still sung during festivals on the Costa Brava.

The first steam ship to go into service was the *Balear*, which had its maiden run to the Balearic Islands in 1833, and a final moment of nautical glory was achieved when *Ictíneo*, a submarine invented by Narcís Montoriol from Figueres, slipped beneath the waves in the port in 1859. A replica sits beside by Port Vell.

Opposite: Columbus points to the open sea
Above: Leisure craft in the port with the old customs house behind

Walk: Port Vell

A boat trip aboard a *Golondrina* ('swallow') around Barcelona's port is a highlight of a visit to the city. Ashore, it is pleasant to wander along the quayside of the Moll de Fusta and Moll d'Espanya where there is always something going on. Often there are tall ships visiting, and you can always guess at the lives of the owners of the luxury yachts in the Marina Port Vell.

Allow two hours.

Start at Drassanes metro (line 3), near the Maritime Museum and end at Barceloneta Metro (line 4).

Columbus looks down on the port

1 World Trade Center
Standing at the end of the Moll de Barcelona, for all the world like one of the visiting passenger liners that draws up alongside it, the World Trade Center is an architectural showcase designed by the American firm of Pei, Cobb, Fred and Partners, who also gave us the glass pyramid outside the Louvre in Paris. There are four eight-storey buildings, three of which are for commercial use, the fourth the five-star Grand Marina Hotel. Also here is Ruccola (*tel: 93 508 82 68*), one of the most fashionable restaurants in the city with top chef, Joan Piqué.

2 Museu Marítim
One of the principal reasons for going to the maritime museum is to look at the Reials Drassanes, the royal dockyards in which the collection of boats, charts and models is housed. It is an extraordinary piece of medieval civic architecture, a row of bays in which galleys were built, then slipped into the water (which now lies a hundred metres or so away). There

is a replica at the Reial, one of the many vast vessels built here, which achieved glory at the Battle of Lepanto.
Plaça Portal de la Pau 1. Tel: 933 18 32 45. Open: 10am–6pm. Admission charge.

3 Monument à Colon
This figure of Christopher Columbus stands in the Plaça Portal de la Pau, the landing stage for the city where the navigator, his wife, three sons, fellow sailors and seven Carib Indians stepped ashore after the triumphant discovery of the Americas. The statue was designed for the Universal Exhibition of 1888 by Gaietà Buïgas i Monravà. A lift takes visitors to a viewing platform near the top of the 60m (200ft) column, which was made in part from melted-down cannon from the castle on Montjuïc.
Open: 9am–8.30pm. Admission charge.

4 Junta d'Obres del Port
The Port Authority building was the reception point for passengers after it was built in 1907 by the engineer Julio Valdés.

5 Moll d'Espanya

The main arm extending into Port Vell houses two yacht clubs and a variety of leisure facilities, including a number of cafeterias and bars situated in the **Maramagnum** mall. There is an IMAX **cinema** and a walkthrough **aquarium**, where you can surround yourself with sharks, rays and many other species of fish.

Tel: 932 21 74 74. Open: 9.30am–9pm, Jul–Aug 9.30am–1pm. Admission charge.

6 Museu d'Història de Catalunya

The museum of the history of Catalonia is sited in the Palau de Mar, the sole surviving warehouses on the Moll de Barceloneta, built by Elies Rogent. The handsome, honey-coloured brick building has restaurants with tables on the Marina Port Vell quayside. The view from the café on the top storey alone is worth the admission charge.

Plaça Pau Vila 3. Tel: 932 25 47 00. Open: Tue–Sat 10am–7pm, Sun & holidays 10am–2.30pm. Admission charge.

TRANSPORT CHOICE

There is a variety of transport choices around the port, apart from the Golondrinas. You can pick up the Rodamolls, articulated vehicles that run around the quays, or you could get a seagull's-eye view from the cable-car, from Torre de Jaume 1 by the World Trade Center on the Moll de Barcelona to the Torre de San Sebastià in Barceloneta.

Diagonal

This arterial road that cuts diagonally across the city is one of the most distinctive avenues in Barcelona. Despite the density of its traffic, broad tree-shaded pavements and notable architecture lend it a certain elegance. Whether you take the soon-to-be-inaugurated tram, or whizz down in the open-air tourist bus, get a glimpse of this angle on Barcelona.

The changing face of the Diagonal

What's in a name?

The name Diagonal is loaded with connotations. Like many places in Barcelona, this street proudly reverted to its Catalan Avinguda Diagonal in 1979, shedding the Castilian Avenida del Generalísimo Franco which had been imposed in 1939 after the dictator's victory in the Civil War. Today the name has taken on a new significance because of its associations with the Diagonal Mar, the thrusting new residential area of Barcelona where the Forum 2004 is being held.

From the top

The cars that flood in to the city every morning along the upper reaches of the Diagonal – from the dormitory towns along the industrial River Llobregat – pass luxury hotels, exclusive residential blocks, a university campus, rank upon rank of office blocks and even a royal palace and a polo club. This is a world apart from the dark, narrow alleyways of the Gothic quarter, or the bustling commerce of the Eixample. Each building is its own island, like the people working or living within them. There is none of the intimate jostle you get in the bars and markets downtown.

The Catalan work ethic is reflected in the abundance of banks

Changing gear

After Plaça Francesc Macià the façades of the elegant 19th-century buildings are warmer, with fine shops at street level

Jean Nouvel's Torre Agbar, a new landmark in the Diagonal

by the sea, passing the latest landmarks like the Jean Nouvel Torre Agbar in the Plaça de les Glòries, and the new technology district 22@.

Diagonal Mar Park showing work in progress

and some key examples of *modernista* architecture. Between Passeig de Gràcia and Pau Claris is the Palau Baró de Quadras, beautifully restored to become the Casa Asia and well worth visiting (*Av Diagonal 373. Open: Tue–Sat 10am–8pm, Sun 10am–2pm. Free admission*). Further on is the Casa Terrades, designed by the same architect Puig i Cadafalch, popularly known as Casa de les Punxes, for its fairy-tale spires.

New horizons
The last stretch of this long straight avenue is the latest to be developed. Slicing through the former industrial district of Poble Nou it leads into Barcelona's brand new residential area

ABOVE THE DIAGONAL

The expression 'above the Diagonal' is loaded with ironic social connotations: those who live on the mountain side of the avenue reputedly regard themselves as a cut above those who live beneath it. It is a dangerous generalisation, though it is true to say that the smarter residential areas, more expensive restaurants and boutiques tend to be above this imaginary dividing line and many of its older residents only venture into the old town when it is opera night at the Liceu. They are part of an urban tribe known as *pijos/pijas* who congregate in the smarter cafeterias like Sandor in Plaça Francesc Macià, a strategic roundabout which marks the point where the modern stretch of Diagonal meets the part that cuts through the blocks of the Eixample.

The organisation of large-scale events has become a tradition in Barcelona's history. The whole world heard about the success of the 1992 Olympics and while the 1888 and 1929 Universal Exhibitions made less impact internationally they certainly left their stamp on the city. True to character, the latest venture is on a vast scale, a first in world history.

No one quite knows how the idea for a Universal Forum of Cultures was first conceived. Rumour has it that during the 1992 Olympics the charismatic former mayor Pasqual Maragall astounded his colleagues by suddenly announcing it as the next major event, a new goal for the city to work towards.

The evolution of Forum 2004 has been plagued with pitfalls and its purpose questioned and criticised. However, jointly organised by the City Council, the Generalitat of Catalonia and the Spanish government, and with the backing of all 186 member countries of UNESCO, it has forged ahead. The show will go on and the name Barcelona will be written even larger on the world map. Apart from the kudos, the city will inherit material benefits like a state-of-the-art conference centre and a brand new marina.

In the prelude to the Forum a completely new residential area has mushroomed next to the site. Known as Diagonal Mar, it consists of high-rise homes with a sea view, several hotels, a park designed by Catalan architect Enric Miralles and the inevitable shopping centre. Like the Olympics, this has been an opportunity for world-class architects to include a piece in the architectural showcase that Barcelona has become. The main Forum building is designed by Swiss architects Herzog and De Meuron.

This is new Barcelona, created largely by property developers and heavyweight investors. The Forum itself is described in startling figures, with 5 million euros to be spent on the opening and closing ceremonies alone. In the 15ha (37 acres) La Plaza, the second largest square in the world after Beijing's Tiananmen Square, 3,500 artists will perform 984 shows daily. Five million real visitors are expected, but a potential 47 million virtual people can follow it and participate on the Internet and another 500 million through the media.

However dazzling the figures, no one can deny the high ideals behind this international event. The millions of visitors expected will be able to participate in debates on the three core themes: cultural diversity, sustainable development and conditions for peace, considered the key issues facing the world in the 21st century. From May to September 2004 exhibitions, festivals, theatre, music, dance, cabaret, circuses, puppet shows, all based around these main themes, will take place in the Forum venue and all around Barcelona.

Opposite: The opening ceremony of Forum 2004 will be an eye-catching spectacle at sea
Above: Virtual view of the side of the Forum building

Eixample

One striking feature of any map of Barcelona is that the majority of its blocks of buildings have their corners knocked off. This is the unique style of the Eixample (the expansion), the 19th-century development that spread dramatically out of the old town and became the springboard for the new architecture – *modernisme*.

Modernista pharmacy

The industrial revolution attracted huge numbers of immigrants to Barcelona in the 19th century, and it soon became clear that not just a few suburbs were needed to cope with this increased population, but a whole new city had to be built. Leaving the old town to its own devices, the city was to extend to fill the plain between the hills of Tibidabo and Montjuïc, and between the Llobregat and Besòs rivers.

Ildefons Cerdà

When architects were invited to submit plans for the new city the town hall chose one drawn up by its own architect, Antoni Rovira i Trias, which envisaged roads radiating out like spokes from the old city. However, the decision was reversed by the authorities in Madrid, who for reasons that were never made clear insisted on another design: one submitted by Ildefons Cerdà i Sunyer (1815–76), a utopian civil engineer and parliamentary deputy who had a walrus moustache and a record of collecting statistical material about the state of the city. His plans, which can be seen in the Museu d'Història de la Ciutat, consisted of row upon row of square grids measuring 133m by 133m (436ft by

436ft) with streets 20m wide. Buildings would occupy two sides of each 'island', allowing for extensive gardens and parks, and the whole area would be crossed by three major avenues, two running diagonally, meeting at Plaça de les Glòries. There would be a total of 550 blocks with angled corners (*xamfrans*), patios and gardens, and everyone would live in harmony: there would be no rich or poor end of town.

Speculators step in

That was the ideal, and in 1860 the first stone of this great plan was laid by Isabella II and the streets given the names of all the heroes in Catalonia's history. But it was more than a decade before the city's economy was in good enough shape for building work really to get under way. When it did start, it happened piecemeal, much of it falling to speculators and unscrupulous landlords. Cerdà's plans were ignored and the parks and green areas built over – except for the Parc de l'Escorxador, now the Parc Joan Miró, signposted by the sculptor's colourful 22m (70ft) *Dona i Ocell* (*Woman and Bird*).

Little by little, however, money came in and allowed for grander houses to be designed. Market forces also came into play to make the area around Avinguda de Gràcia and the right side of the new railway running inland from Plaça Catalunya more desirable than the land on the left side of the tracks. It was on the left side that the first major public building in the Eixample was constructed in 1872 – the university, designed by Elies

Rogent i Amat. The right side, the *dreta*, was where the showcase houses were built. The height limitation on buildings was raised.

The Quadrat d'Or

The generation of architects who came after Cerdà were not imbued with the same utopian socialism, and many of them saw the grids of the original plan as a constraint on human endeavour. By the time they were on the scene in the 1890s they began to pull down some of the first buildings to create bigger and better homes, particularly around the Passeig de Gràcia, creating a 'Quadrat d'Or', a golden square of *modernista* excellence. Bordered by Plaça Catalunya, Carrer de Aribau, Avinguda de Diagonal and Passeig Saint Joan, this area of around 100 blocks has the highest concentration of *modernista* buildings in the city, with works by most of its great practitioners. Among them is the former publishing house on Editorial Montaner i Simon in Carrer d'Aragó. Designed by the owner's brother,

Fundació Antoní Tapiès in the Quadrat d'Or, by Domènech i Montaner

Lluís Domènech i Montaner, in 1879 it was the first private buiding in the city to use an ironwork structure. It is now a gallery for Catalonia's best known contemporary artist, Antoni Tàpies (*see p134*). Many are now commercial premises, with some of the city's smartest shops, but a number were built as apartment blocks.

The last chapter

Cerdà's plans, which had such an impact on the city, have adapted and mellowed over the years, depending on taste, need and city fortunes. The story ends with Forum 2004 (*see pp58–9*) when the Diagonal finally does Cerdà's bidding and reaches all the way down to the sea.

BENEATH THE STREETS

Cerdà's plans for the city were based on an ideal of giving the people of Barcelona better housing, and that included better health and sanitation. The first Sanitation Plan was completed by the engineer Pere Garcia Faria in 1891, and it can be see in the Eixample's **Museu del Clavegueram** (Sewage Museum – *Passeig Sant Joan 98. Tel: 934 57 65 50 for an appointment for a tour of the city sewers*). The museum covers 900m² (9,700sq ft) and looks at the city's essential waterworks from Roman times to the large-scale works carried out for the Olympic Games of 1992.

Two of the famous trio of *modernista* buildings in Passeig de Gràcia, by Puig i Cadafalch (left) and Gaudí

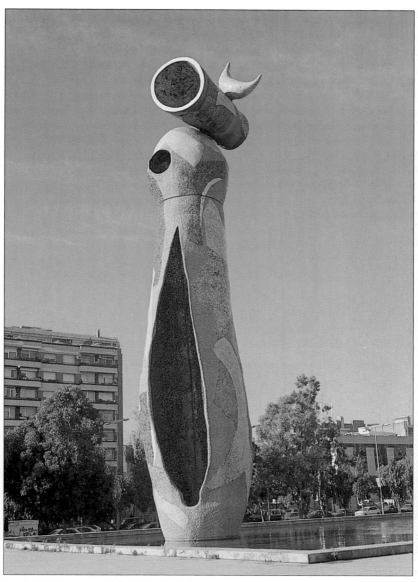

Joan Miró's 'Woman and Bird' in The Parc de l'Escorxador, once the site of slaughterhouses

Barcelona's unique gift to architecture is a style it developed over successive generations of architects who shaped the city from around 1880 to 1930. It has its counterparts in the English Arts and Crafts movement, in French Art Nouveau and in Austrian Jugendstil. But it also had its own inspiration in Catalan Gothic and the *mudéjar* style of Islam.

When the city broke down its medieval walls and took up the plans for an extension (Eixample, *see pp60–63*), there was plenty of room for creativity and development. But it was not until the Universal Exhibition of 1888 that a new local style could be detected. The exhibition was held in the recently landscaped Parc de la Ciutadella (*see pp102–3*). A keynote was set by Josep Vilaseca's Arc de Triomf, but of greater impact was the work of a popular 38-year-old professor from Barcelona

University's School of Architecture, Lluís Domènech i Montaner. For visitors to the exhibition he designed the Gran Hotel Internacional to cater for 1,000 guests, and had it built by the port in just 53 days. Nobody could ignore such panache.

For the exhibition he designed the Café-Restaurant based on the medieval stock exchange in Valencia. With intricate brick and ironwork, it was dismissed by many critics as backward-looking, but the architect wanted to find local influences for the modern buildings and in so doing he begun what was later seen as the *nova scuola catalana*. After the exhibition closed Domènech used the northeast tower of the building (now the Museu Zoològic) as a workshop to develop ironwork, ceramic tiles, stained glass and stone carving, all of which played an immensely important part in the movement that followed.

Domènech's further contributions to the city included the dazzling Palau de la Música Catalana (*see p44*) and the monumental Hospital de la Santa Creu i de Sant Pau, both exquisite examples of *modernisme*. His most successful pupil was Josep Puig i Cadafalch, who was just 15 years old when he gazed in awe at the giant hotel rising on the waterfront. Leading light of the succeeding generation of *modernista* architects, his designs were more conservative, but they included Plaça Catalunya and the 1929 Universal Exhibition in Montjuïc.

Both Domènech and Puig were also active political figures. *Modernista* design was tied to a rising sense of nationalism, of wanting something that was particularly Catalan. The Renaixença, a renaissance of Catalonia, was in full spate. There was money from South America and the industrial revolution to create patrons such as Eusebi Güell, and *modernista* architecture was applied to many commercial and industrial buildings.

Modernisme is not an easy term to attach to the variety of styles that were created during these few decades. Certainly Gaudí did not want to be associated with such liberal frivolity, and it blends into *noucentisme*, the style that followed it. But the three architects' neighbouring works in Passeig de Gràcia – Domènech's Casa Lléo Morera, Puig's Casa Amatller and Gaudí's Casa Batlló (*see p68*) – show just how different and exciting the times were in which they lived.

Opposite: Casa Milà
Above: Coloured ceramic mosaics were an integral part of *modernista* houses

Walk: Passeig de Gràcia and Rambla Catalunya

The only way to appreciate *modernista* architecture fully is to wander around the streets of the Eixample, looking up at roof details, spotting decorative balconies, pausing in doorways to admire the tiling or some elaborate staircase. This walk up and down the two main streets of the district allows you to do just that, taking in some of the key buildings of that era, as well as getting the feel of the elegant heart of contemporary Barcelona.

Allow 1–2 hours (not including pauses for coffee, visits to buildings or shopping, all of which you will be tempted to do). From Plaça Catalunya walk up Passeig de Gràcia and cross Gran Via.

1 J. Roca

This jewellery shop was designed in 1934 by a young Josep Lluís Sert, close friend of artist Joan Miró. It is one of the few pieces he built in Barcelona

La Pedrera, Gaudí's revolutionary apartment block

before going into exile in the USA after the Civil War. He designed the Spanish Republican Pavilion for the 1937 Paris International Exhibition where Picasso's Guernica was first exhibited and after Franco's death returned to build the magnificent Miró Foundation on Montjuïc.

2 Lamp-post

A trademark of Passeig de Gràcia, these wrought-iron lamp-posts designed by municipal architect Pere Falqués in 1906 must be some of the most beautiful in the world, and some of the few you can sit under. They can be spotted all the way up this handsome avenue which once joined Barcelona to the former village of Gràcia. Notice the Gaudí hexagonal pavement tiles, which are now for sale in smart souvenir shops.

Bird's-eye view of Passeig de Gràcia

3 Illa de la Discòrdia

Cross over Consell de Cent, a street full of art galleries and fashion, and you arrive at the Casa Lleó Morera (*No 35*), the first in this block known as the 'Block of Discord' because of its discordant styles of *modernista* architecture. The three main houses are by the key architects of the period. The first is the work of Domènech i Montaner, showing his decorative detailing especially in the wonderful ceramic work in the entrance hall. Further up at No 41 is the Casa Amatller by Puig i Cadafalch with his distinctive neo-Gothic style, and currently the centre for the *Ruta del Modernisme* (a do-it-yourself guided tour of *modernisme* in the city). And next door is the unmistakable hand of Gaudí in the Casa Batlló with its extravagant dream-like façade and flowing interior. The house was opened to the public in 2002, and the policy will hopefully continue. No opportunity to visit this extraordinary house should be missed. *See also pp64–5 & pp110–11.*

4 Casa Milà

Continue up the street and you will find the Casa Milà, one of Gaudí's most famous buildings. Popularly known as La Pedrera ('the Quarry') for its roughly honed façade, this apartment block was built in 1910. Despite the queues it is worth visiting for a deeper insight into Gaudí, for its spectacular roof terrace, for *El Pis*, a show flat decorated as a period piece, and for the sheer beauty of it. It is owned and maintained by local bank the Caixa de Catalunya, whose exhibition space on the first floor has a programme of quality art exhibitions. *Open: daily 10am–8pm.*

5 Casa de Ramon Casas

The house at No 96 was the home and studio of *modernista* painter Ramon Casas. His work can be seen in the Museu d'Art Modern in the Parc de la Ciutadella. The house has a higher profile today as the home of Vinçon, selling everything for the home from corkscrews to couches, a mecca for the design-conscious. Slip into the patio from its first floor for a glimpse of Casas' studio and to get an idea of the typical patio of the Eixample blocks.

6 Palau Robert

Across the road, just before Avinguda Diagonal, is the Tourist Information Centre for Catalonia. The shady gardens behind are peaceful and a pleasant short cut through to Còrsega and on to Rambla de Catalunya.

7 Casa Serra

The original house built by Puig i Cadafalch in 1908 was adapted to accommodate the Diputació de Barcelona, the body representing Spain's central government, in the 1980s with an ingenious modern extension by influential Olympic architects Milà and Correa. From here the elegant length of Rambla Catalunya stretches down to Plaça Catalunya. Since the mid-19th century it has been the classic avenue for strolling down, pausing for a refreshing *orxata* and people-watching. This is the place to spot the bourgeois Catalans, immaculately coiffed and dressed, walking their dogs or grandchildren and meeting friends.

8 Passatge de la Concepció

One of several passageways with pretty terraced houses and sometimes gardens *a la inglesa* that cut through the typical Eixample block. Passatge Permanyer between Pau Claris and Roger de Llúria is another attractive example. Somewhat exclusive as homes, this one is known for its trendy and stylish 'sister' restaurants, Tragaluz and El Japonés, and leads back to Passeig de Gràcia.

9 Maurí

On the crossroads with Provença are two flagship Catalan establishments. Maurí is a desirable pastry shop and delicatessen, where silver-haired ladies meet for lunch or *berenar* (an afternoon snack). On the opposite *xamfran* (corner) is Groc, the original Toni Miró shop, wonderfully low-key for the birthplace of an empire.

10 Fundació Tàpies

Cross Aragó and look back at the Tàpies Foundation for a better appreciation of this building. Apart from the large

collection of Tàpies' work its temporary exhibitions are high-quality. Housed in a former publishing firm designed by Domènech i Montaner, it is crowned by an original Tàpies sculpture *Núvol i Cadira* (*Cloud and Chair*).
Open: Tue–Sun 10am–8pm. See p134.

11 Galeria Joan Prats

Just below Aragó on the left is one of the city's oldest and most famous art galleries, Joan Prats, known for its exhibitions of leading contemporary art. Its beautiful painted glass frontage is just one of many on Rambla Catalunya, like the elegant ironmonger's next door. On the other side of the road is the Casa Miquel Fargas, a suitably decorative setting for Muxart, the shoe shop. Designed by Catalan Hermenegildo Muxart, these wildly creative shoes are works of art.
From here continue down Rambla Catalunya until it meets Plaça Catalunya, after which it becomes the more famous La Rambla that leads to the port. Alternatively take Consell de Cent and head back to Passeig de Gràcia and the metro.

The impressive chimneys on the roof of Casa Milà

Designer Barcelona

These two words have been irrevocably linked since the surge of activity in the 1980s, when pent-up creative energy was unleashed with the return of democracy in Spain. It was particularly marked in Catalonia, then fuelled by the Olympic Games in 1992. The momentum has continued into the 21st century, with 2003 designated the Year of Design in Barcelona.

But this is hardly a new phenomenon. There is an undeniable creative streak running through Catalan blood. Gaudí was not just a genius but wildly creative. And look at the industrialist Güell who was daring enough to be his patron. The whole *modernista* movement depended on the support of the Catalan

bourgeoisie. Catalans are not afraid to stand out of line – in fact they are delighted to be different from the more conservative Madrid. They also have an innate sense of style – in their dress, homes and offices, designer labels are the thing. Hence the success of establishments like Vinçon, a design emporium on Passeig de Gràcia which manages to sell a tablemat as a designer item. Nearby is another interiors shop, possibly the most beautiful in Barcelona, BD Ediciones de Diseño (*Mallorca 291*). Selling the best of 20th-century design its own interior won an award in 1979 for its renovation, within Domènech i Montaner's Casa Thomas.

The boom time in the 1980s saw the opening of the famous designer bars, most of which are still open: Nick Havanna (*Rosselló 208*), Universal (*Marià Cubí 184*), Otto Zutz, the designer disco (*Lincoln 15*), Zsa Zsa (*Rosselló 156*). At the same time Barcelona became the centre of the fashion industry in Spain, led by Antonio Miró who remains supreme even though he has diversified into accessories like briefcases and also black bathroom suites. Younger designers like Josep Font, Josep Abril, David Valls have also made an impact on the international scene. And in the world of advertising Barcelona agencies started to bring home the top creative awards from international festivals.

Just as the establishment had sponsored the *modernista* architects at the start of the 20th century, and the new Eixample was a showcase of Barcelona's creativity, so did the authorities encourage the design movement in the aftermath of Franco. It became an integral part of their ambitious plans for the city. Dynamic mayor Pasqual Maragall and his city council were instrumental in the dramatic changes to Barcelona, using the Olympic Games as a catalyst to execute long-overdue projects for the city which, as the promotional campaigns said at the time, would benefit the citizens of Barcelona in the future. Even the Games were 'Designer Olympics', from the Toni Miró uniforms to Javier Mariscal's mascot 'Cobi'. Sculptures by national and international artists appeared in newly created squares and parks that opened up dense inner city districts. A new airport was built by Ricardo Bofill, complete with designer palm trees. Designer Barcelona was on display in 1992 for millions of visitors and TV screens, but, as the slogans promised, the Barcelonans are the lucky ones who carry on living in it.

Opposite: Furniture design is just one of the many design elements in Barcelona
Left: A giant prawn, typical of Javier Mariscal's light-hearted touch
Below: Rear view of Cobi, the first designer – Olympic mascot

Gràcia

Slightly off the tourist track, the city district of Gràcia and its socially cohesive community offers a real slice of atmospheric Mediterranean life. So far untouched by major development projects, it is also home to a delightful early building by Gaudí.

Plaça Rius i Taulet

Stretching up to the Park Güell above the Diagonal, Gràcia was formerly a town in its own right (it was annexed by Barcelona in 1897) and has always kept its distinctive identity and personality. Residents are proud to be *Graciencs* first and Barcelonans second. Many of Gràcia's place names like Carrer de la Fraternitat, Plaça de la Revolució, Mercat de la Llibertat, bear witness to the town's reputation as a centre of radical activity, while recent additions to the people's-hero tradition are squares named after John Lennon and Anne Frank.

Gràcia Village begins at the top of Passeig de Gràcia

The neighbourhood is a criss-cross of narrow streets studded with tree-shaded squares that serve as social centres, perfect for lounging on café terraces and people-watching: you may well see locals in dressing gowns and slippers popping out for a loaf of freshly baked bread or the morning paper. Still a bastion of artisans and small family businesses, Gràcia has a well-integrated gypsy community and its cheap old premises are a haven for the New Age movement.

Time warp

In sightseeing terms, the highlight of Gràcia is the surprising Casa Vicens, Gaudí's early Moorish-style building tucked away unpretentiously in the narrowest of streets. While the main shopping streets like Gran de Gràcia, Travessera de Gràcia, and Torrent de l'Olla are busy day and night, many of the side streets are pedestrianised and peaceful. Old-fashioned shops in dark cluttered premises rub shoulders with big-name franchises, designer boutiques with junk shops, alternative therapy centres with gaudy bargain bazaars. Here locals queue around the block for dried chickpeas and lentils, spit-roasted chickens and cut-price underwear. Unique establishments suspended in a blissful time warp before Barcelona's obsession with retail design are still to be found, like the Ferreteria Soriano at Gran de Gràcia 53, with its antiquated display windows jammed with every kitchen utensil the human mind could conceive of.

Vibrant

The long Carrer Verdi is one of the hubs of Gràcia's vibrant cultural scene and night-life, attracting people from all over Barcelona. Activities include social events and handicrafts workshops, alternative and mainstream theatre, cinemas showing subtitled (not dubbed) films, clubs and bars, and eateries serving everything from the rustic Catalan tomato-scraped doorsteps of bread with ham and sausages to first-class seafood, pizzas and late-night Moroccan and Lebanese dishes.

Summer festival

Creative imagination is something that Gràcia shares with Gaudí. The summer extravaganza, the *festa major* or annual town festival, in mid-August draws thousands from across the city.

Residents' committees spend the best part of the year drawing up and executing their plans for the Best Street competition, for which entire streets are transformed into themed settings: science fiction worlds, medieval towns, Jurassic parks, Moorish gardens... Each group of streets organises its own non-stop programme of entertainments such as chess and dominoes tournaments, children's chocolate parties and puppet shows, foam machines and street discos.

Stages are set up in the squares for dancing to live salsa and rock late into the night.

Gràcia is characterised by small squares, many of which have been renovated and landscaped

Walk: Gràcia

Gràcia was formerly a thriving town, and was annexed to Barcelona in 1897. Quiet narrow streets and big shady squares form the fabric of what is one of the city's most dynamic and popular neighbourhoods.

Allow 2–3 hours including browsing and stops for rest and refreshment.

The walk begins at Fontana metro station on Gràcia's main street, reached by metro line 3 or the 22, 24 or 28 bus.

1 Casa Vicens

The street is so narrow that it is impossible to get a panoramic view of this colourful turreted little castle (1883–8), the only house designed by Gaudí to have been lived in by generations of the original family without a break until the present day (not open to visitors). Gaudí's first work, it was inspired by Gothic and Moorish architecture.

2 Plaça Ana Frank

Renovated in 2001, this small square is graced with a statue of Anne Frank lying pensively, diary in hands, face-down on the projecting roof of the Gràcia Crafts and Civic Centre. The mosaic on the wall behind it is by the Escola Massana, Barcelona's school of art and design. The square now seems to be more of a monument to spray-paint urban art than to anything else.

3 Plaça del Sol

Rebuilt in the 1990s to accommodate an underground car park, this square is one of Gràcia's nerve centres, in particular frequented by young people at night.

Shade from ancient overhanging trees is a boon in the hot summer. Gràcia still preserves some rather beautiful old buildings like the one on the corner of Carrer Virtut (the excellent Envalira restaurant is on the ground floor) with façade in green and white *esgrafiat*, a form of decoration very typical of Catalunya.

4 Plaça Rius i Taulet

Down across the Travessera, one of the main commercial arteries, is Gràcia's main square, with its original Town Hall (now the Municipal District Headquarters) at the bottom end. The clock tower was built in 1864. This is where Barcelona officially (on TV) sees in the New Year. The café terraces are perfect for resting and people-watching.

5 Plaça de la Revolució de Septembre de 1868

Several narrow streets take you across Torrent de l'Olla, a busy shopping street, past Gràcia's main market and back up to a square which is really a place of passage, although benches under trees afford rest. The green façade of No 24, at the bottom end, is a good example of the *esgrafiat* style. The square is the gateway to the popular Carrer Verdi, a pedestrianised street packed with ethnic shops and restaurants. The building at the corner of Carrer Vallfogona is particularly quirky and ornate.

6 Plaça de la Virreina
Bustling Verdi leads, via the Carrer de l'Or, to this peaceful square with the plain, soothing façade of the church of Sant Joan de Gràcia. From here you can pop along the Carrer Asturies, this section of which is a cool tunnel of leafy trees, to the emblematic Plaça del Diamant, the setting of the best-known Catalan novel of the same name (*see p25*).

The fame of Barcelona by night has spread far and wide, not without due cause. As a result it has unfortunately become a top venue for stag nights amongst northern Europeans – who have not grasped how the locals do nightlife, gliding through with no apparent sign of intoxication and amazingly able to appear at work early the next morning.

The *Madrileños* may argue that Barcelona is tame compared with a night out in the capital city, but for most of us it is quite wild. The first important thing to understand is that nothing really gets going until after 1am. The early evening is just preamble. Whether you begin with a chilled wine in a Gothic square, a cool beer in the bustling Plaça del Sol in Gràcia, or a tapa in one of the many Basque theme bars to have opened recently, the choice is wide before dinner – which does not happen until after 9pm.

The evening can turn into night in the after-dinner bars which remain open until 2 or 3am. End the evening now and you can get a comparatively early night. It is difficult, though, to resist the temptation to go on, especially on summer nights when the night cool is the best time to be on the streets, as most of Barcelona seems to be. Around this time the clubs and discos start to get into gear. Long-standing discos like Otto Zutz (*Lincoln 15*) or the small Club Dot (*Nou de Sant Francesc 7*) are still good value, but are being outshone by venues which often have live music earlier in the evening then metamorphose into clubs with a DJ after 2 or 3am. Most popular are the Apollo (*Nou de la Rambla*), Cibeles (*Córsega 363*) and the eternal La Paloma (*Tigre 27*), a turn-of-the-century dance hall dripping in gilt and red velvet banquettes. Razzmatazz (*Pamplona 88*) has a lively concert and DJ programme in its three different spaces all within an old warehouse in Poble Nou. A favourite in the summer is La Terraza in Poble Espanyol with its outdoor dance floor and cool crowd.

Some of the annual festivals feature special programming in the night, like Sonar for Advanced Music, every June, and the popular fiestas of the different *barris*, notably in Gràcia in mid-August and the main Barcelona fiesta of La Mercè in September when concerts in the squares of the Old Town may not begin until midnight. The Grec Summer Festival where most shows begin at 10pm now has an After-Grec with performances beginning after the main programming ends. There is only one solution – try a siesta.

Opposite: One of La Paloma's late night DJ sessions
Above: A multi-space club for concerts and dance

Plaça Catalunya and La Rambla

Many towns and cities in Spain have a *rambla*, a tree-lined avenue where a stream or river once seasonally flowed. But none are as well known or as entertaining as La Rambla in Barcelona. Running from Plaça Catalunya to the port, the city's most famous highway is a slice of history and a place of continual diversions.

Miró pavement, La Rambla

Monument to Macià, much-loved President of the Generalitat in the 1930s

Plaça Catalunya

La Rambla begins at Plaça Catalunya, where the old town meets the new. Beneath this broad square, laid out in 1927, is a major railway station, a metro station and a central information point. The square is a gathering place for demonstrations and a focus of events on La Diada, Catalonia's national day (11 September). Near the metro exit is a contemporary sculpture of Francesc Macià, who boldly declared Catalonia independent shortly before the Civil War. The work is by Josep Maria Subirachs, who sculpted the angular figures on the Passion façade of the Sagrada Família.

The best-known of the many commercial premises that surround the square is **El Corte Inglés** department store, which has a fifth-floor restaurant with good views over the city.

On the southwest corner of the square is the **Café Zurich**, a historic café which, like a number of places in the Rambla, figures in *Homage to Catalonia*, George Orwell's classic story of the Civil War. It was built in 1927 as the railway's café and became a haunt of writers and chess players. During a recent major overhaul of this corner facing the Rambla it was rebuilt, but its interior remains authentic and it makes a good meeting spot.

La Rambla

Theoretically there is not one but five Ramblas (Les Rambles in Catalan, Las Ramblas in Castilian – but the singular, La Rambla, works in both languages). Today there is still a distinct flavour to each of these five sections that make up the street.

The river, the Cagallel, which had its source in the Collserola hills and dried up in summer, was converted into an underground sewer in the 14th century, by which time the city walls ran its

La Boqueria, a cathedral of food, is the main market in the old town

whole length, on the northern (Ciutat Vella) side. From the 16th century a number of large convents were built on the opposite side of the street, giving their names to the **Rambla Santa**

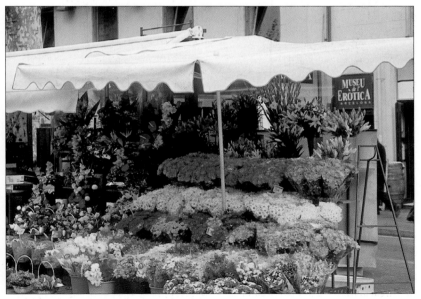

Flower stalls, beautifully arranged and popular with Barcelonans, are a great attraction of La Rambla

Mònica, **Rambla St Josep** and **Rambla de la Capputxins**, and resulting in the street being nicknamed 'Via Conventa'.

Grand houses and hotels

In the late 18th century Jaume I's city walls began to be pulled down, and the Rambla was straightened into an avenue. Large mansions such as the **Palau de la Virreina**, **Palau Moja** and **Casa March de Reus** were built to show off their owners' wealth. More dramatically, in 1835, Sant Josep and a college of Barefoot Trinitarians were among several religious houses burned one night by a dissatisfied mob after a disappointing bullfight, leaving space for the **La Boqueria** covered market and the **Liceu** opera house to be built. Other monastic buildings were put out of use when four-fifths of the city's church land was sold off under government decree later the same year. Monastic traces can be seen in several buildings in the street, notably the **Oriente**, **Sant Agustí** and **Peninsular hotels** and in the **Centre d'Art Santa Mònica**.

Twenty years after the *desamortació* of

At the kiosks you will find newspapers, books, maps and postcards the religious houses, all the fortifications had been torn down, opening up the Rambla to the old town. Plane trees were introduced, gas lighting installed and the Rambla became one of the most talked-about thoroughfares in Europe.

Famous visitors

The fame of the thoroughfare began to spread. George Sand wrote of 'coquettish' women with their tremulous fans, and men who seemed unconcerned about anything that happened outside the city. It certainly was always a place for night owls. Staying on the Rambla a century later Rose Macaulay complained that she was woken at four in the morning by loud conversation. In *Fabled Shore* (1949), she wrote, 'Going out on my balcony and looking down I perceived that the Rambla was still full of people sitting at café tables or on seats beneath trees, or strolling to and fro, talking, laughing and screaming with the greatest vivacity, the street lights that gleamed above the plane trees now paling a little in the dawn.'

Today the Rambla extends down into the old port with an added **Rambla del Mar** bridging the water to The Moll d'Espanya. The seediness of the waterfront has disappeared, and the whole street is always a pleasant place to stroll.

Having your picture drawn is one of many ways of being diverted along the Rambla

On certain evenings from September to June an unfamiliar ripple runs down La Rambla around 8pm. There is an expensive smell in the air, and more than the usual number of men in suits and fur-coated ladies can be spotted emerging out of the metro. Silver-grey saloon cars with tinted windows queue to get into car parks. There is no mistaking the signs – it is opera night at the Gran Teatre del Liceu.

Bastion of the Catalan bourgeoise, this opera house on La Rambla has had a variegated history since its bizarre origins in the 1830s as an amateur operatic group known as the Liceo Filodramático de Montesión whose purpose was to raise funds for a battalion of soldiers. They used to perform in an abandoned convent, the Montsió, until, flushed with success and evolving into a purely artistic group, they needed more space. In 1847 a grand

new opera house on the scale of Milan's La Scala was inaugurated on the site of another former convent on La Rambla. In other European cities the opera was often sponsored by the monarchy, but the Liceu was funded by rich Catalan industrialists, and boxes were sold for life to the affluent families of Barcelona. Its first opera was Donizetti's *Anna Bolena*, but at that time performances included dance, concerts, musical comedies, plays and magic shows.

The first dramatic event in its turbulent history was in 1861 when fire destroyed the stage and auditorium, but phoenix-like it quickly reopened in 1862. Then followed a period of growth during which the distinctive divisions of Catalan society were clearly seen in the theatre's layout: the stalls and boxes were the domain of the elegantly dressed bourgeoisie while the higher seats and the gods were crammed with the lower echelons, who could barely see the stage. However it was a time of social and political unrest and this apparent peaceful cohabitation was shaken when an anarchist threw a bomb into the stalls on the opening night of the season in 1893, killing about 20 people.

The latest incident was in 1994 when a dramatic blaze leapt out of the

Liceu's roof on a January morning to the amazement of passers-by. Apparently caused by a welder's spark, it quickly took hold of the ancient wooden structure that had long been due for renovation. Just as in 1861 the Catalan authorities, weighty bodies and faithful bourgeoisie rallied around and five years later a new Gran Teatre del Liceu was born, designed by the much acclaimed local architect Ignasi Solà Morales. Contrary to the wishes of many who saw it as an opportunity to build a showcase of new Catalan architecture, it is an extremely expensive reproduction of the old theatre with indulgent finishes, dripping in gilt, swathed in velvet and lined with marble. There are no surprises, though some pleasing quirky features like the ceiling designed by contemporary artist Perejaume, and stage curtains by fashion designer Antonio Miró. It is also a long-overdue technological marvel with two stages able to cope with simultaneous performances.

As for its spirit, the new Liceu is more daring artistically, collaborating with avant-garde theatre companies like the Fura dels Baus. It has also initiated a policy of *òpera per tothom* in a bid to make opera available to a wider section of society, with more productions at affordable prices as well as foyer and children's performances.

Left: The façade of the opera house was not affected by the fire in 1994
Above: The glossy and glamorous rebuilt interior of the Liceu

From the moment it leaves Plaça Catalunya till it disgorges its flow of human traffic by the port, La Rambla is a constant parade of colourful characters. Apart from the transient street artists who are ruled by the weather, fashion or the state of their income, there is an assortment of perennial characters who are part of the very fabric of La Rambla. Famous for over 150 years as a place to promenade, it is now acquiring a new label as one of the longest theatres in the world.

Topping the bill and with regular appearances all the way down are the newspaper vendors in their distinctive green news-stands. Day and night whatever the weather they stand grimly

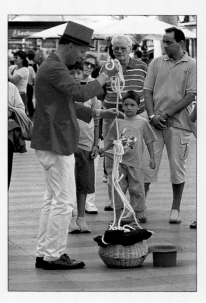

surveying the scene and always at the ready with the latest news. Also near the top is the intellectual shoe-shiner. Bronzed like a chestnut, when he is not squatting at someone's feet this wise Peruvian is reading the leaders in *El Pais* newspaper. Gathered around the entrance to the metro station at *aperitivo* time, or early evening, are crowds of retired men, twittering like sparrows, having a *tertulia*, an ingrained Spanish tradition of gathering together to discuss politics, football and putting the world to rights.

Human statues are the latest wave of performers in this elongated theatre. Some are highly professional, like the Jack-in-the-Box whose legs have disappeared but he still does not blink, or the metal cowboy standing on a wall by the Liceu metro. Others take the prize for humour, like the pink-haired lady in a leopard-skin coat who has been felled by a boulder on her way to the opera, or for sheer endurance – the increasingly pregnant 19th-century silver lady with her top-hatted partner.

The mobile performers are another inconsistent art form. Amongst the excellent is the South American with his concert-pianist frog. There are break-dancers, guitarists, a funky jazz musician with his piano on wheels – but the prize goes to the latest in fusion, a flamenco dancer who stamps on his *tablao* (portable dance floor) to the accompaniment of didgeridoos.

Beware the less desirable characters and rogues. The worst are the *trilleros* who invite you to guess which carrot-top the bean is under. With their stooges in the crowd they make it look simple, but no one ever beats them. At the first whistle from a lookout they disappear into thin air as the police cruise into sight only to find a bunch of gaping tourists. Pickpockets are another hazard, and find good fodder among the madding crowds distracted by one of the many acts.

In the last stretch are the literal artists, lined up to sketch your caricature or sell their works of art. And as a grand finale is Colon, the tallest statue of them all, never yet been known to blink.

Opposite: Street characters pulling in the crowds
Above and below: Human statues are the latest addition to the many characters found in La Rambla

Walk: Strolling down La Rambla

It would be foolish to try and go down Europe's most famous boulevard in any other way. Strolling is the way to do it, as the crush of people prevents brisk walking and you would be in danger of missing something in this ever-changing colourful spectacle. Go with the flow but take time to notice some of the sites outlined here.

Allow 1–2 hours so there is time to watch street performers, wander around La Boqueria market and maybe even pose as a model for an artist. Begin at the Café Zurich on the corner of Plaça Catalunya or the metro exit at the top of La Rambla.

1 Font de Canaletes
This first stretch is named after its famous 19th-century cast-iron fountain loaded with symbolism for Barcelonans. A small plaque advises that anyone drinking from it will fall in love with the

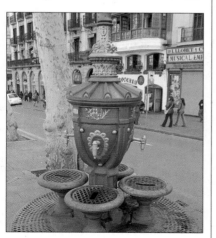

Drink here and you will return to Barcelona

city and inevitably return. Of Barcelona's many fountains this is the only one with a low-lying spring for dogs. Always popular as a meeting place, its noisiest moments are when FC Barcelona has won the cup or the league and its over-excited fans assemble here to celebrate, chanting and blowing horns.

2 Reial Acadèmia de Ciències i Arts
Designed by Josep Domènech i Estapà at the end of the 19th century, this is still the headquarters of the Royal Academy of Science and Arts, and responsible for the Fabra Observatory on Tibidabo. For many years the clock was Barcelona's official timekeeper. Also housed here is the Teatre Poliorama which has a good weekend programme of children's theatre.

3 Palau Moja
This elegant 18th-century neoclassical palace, taken over by the Department of

The fresh produce is a spectacle in La Boqueria

Culture of the Generalitat, unfortunately can only be visited when it is hosting an exhibition. Much of its decorative detailing both exterior and interior can be glimpsed from La Rambla. Recently a major international sportswear brand has taken over the adjoining building, once the palace's garden, which along with the ubiquitous McDonald's on the corner of Ferran spell globalisation and threaten the beginning of the end of La Rambla.

4 Palau de la Virreina

Built in 1778 for the Viceroy of Peru to be ready for his return from Lima. He died soon after, which is why it became known as the Palace of the Vicereine, his widow. Today it provides office space for the Institut de Cultura, the municipal cultural body. Its exhibition spaces on the ground floor and first floor have an active programme, and there is an extremely useful information service open to the public with leaflets on nearly everything going on culturally in the city, and a ticket office. It has a stylish souvenir shop, *La Botiga*, where potential presents are strictly tasteful.

5 La Boqueria

Also known as Mercat de Sant Josep, this is an essential stop on any itinerary. Dating from 1840, it is regarded as the most popular and colourful of Barcelona's many markets (*see pp152–3*) and along with Mercat Santa Caterina claims to be the oldest. Around 300 stalls spill over with fresh food, local vegetables, freshly picked ripe fruit and recently caught seafood. The intoxicating atmosphere of colours, aromas and ceaseless chatter are far more likely to make people return to Barcelona than the legendary water of Canaletes. Recent restoration work has highlighted its fine iron structure, *modernista* details and stained glass. *Open: Mon–Sat early in the morning–8pm.*

6 Casa Bruno Quadras

There are few examples of *modernista* architecture in the Old Town, but this is one of the most attractive. Designed by Josep Vilaseca in 1891, the decorative exterior shows clear signs of the oriental influence which left its mark on many *modernista* architects. Do not miss the umbrella.

7 Gran Teatre del Liceu

The opera house with its dramatic history of fire and bombing is in full splendour since reopening in 1999 (*see* pp82–3). The old façade remains but its new casing now stretches down a whole block on La Rambla and back into the streets Sant Pau and Unió. The opera season has been extended including more dance and children's programmes. *Ticket booking: 902 53 33 53 or from abroad +34 93 274 64 11. www.liceubarcelona.com. Tours daily 10am–1pm.*

8 Plaça Reial

A small opening on the left leads into the magnificent yet notorious Plaça Reial, built between 1848 and 1859, and supposedly inspired by Napoleonic French urban architecture. The elegance of its rigid geometric design and noble palm trees form a curious counterpoint to its decadent atmosphere and shady deals. Beware of pickpockets but be sure to visit it for a drink or a meal in one of the terrace cafés. It comes to life at night when retro bars like Glaciar regain their former *simpatico* atmosphere, and music bar Sidecar or jazz club Jamboree offer a good programme of live gigs. Los Tarantos is one of the most authentic flamenco clubs in town. In the side streets off the square are various laid-back lounge clubs. All life is here.

9 Palau Güell

Gaudí's loyal patron Eusebi Güell commissioned a town house from the architect in 1885 on a site just off La Rambla in Nou de la Rambla. Its façade may be overbearing to some, but once inside the beauty of its details is breathtaking. The world of fantasy on its roof should not be missed. *Nou de la Rambla. Open: Mon–Fri 10am–2pm,*

4–7.30pm. It is compulsory to go on a guided tour, so get there early to book a time.

10 Centre d'Art Santa Mònica

The final stretch of La Rambla is named after the convent which stood on the right, today strikingly converted into an exhibition centre. At street level is the cultural information centre of the Catalan government, with news about what is on in the arts in the whole of Catalonia. The narrow street Santa Mònica, once the stamping ground of the Barri Xino's famous prostitutes, now has a sushi bar but manages to retain a bohemian atmosphere thanks to the evocative Bar Pastís, which has been playing the likes of Piaf and Jacques Brel since the 1950s.

The Palau de la Virreina houses the municipal cultural information centre

Montjuïc

The Olympic flame
burned here in 1992

One of the distinguishing features of Barcelona, marking
the gateway to the south, this bulky hill only 213m (700ft)
high makes its presence felt almost everywhere in the city.
Regenerated twice in the last 100 years as a venue for major
international events, it nevertheless is still underused by
local people. Its latest lease of life is coming from a new
scheme, backed by the City Council, to open up neglected
parts of the hill and make it more accessible so as to
encourage more use of this large green space.

History
A pre-Roman civilization lived here, and
the Romans themselves built a temple to
Jupiter on the hill, which could explain
its name, a derivation of Mons Iovis.
An alternative theory relates the name
to the fact there was a Jewish cemetery
here. The first serious landscaping of
the hill was in preparation for the 1929
Universal Exposition, when many of

The Trade Fair grounds spread out below the
Palau Nacional

today's monumental buildings were
constructed. Some, like the Palau
de Victòria Eugenia and the Palau
d'Alfons XIII, are used by the Barcelona
Trade Fair, while the Palau Nacional
dominating the hilltop has been the
home of the national art museum since
1934, now known as the MNAC (*see
p101*). The stadium over the hill behind
the Palau Nacional was also built for
the event, then refurbished and enlarged
to cope with the next major event to
take place on the hill, the XXV Olympiad
in 1992.

Revival
The Barcelona Olympics may have
been talked about *ad nauseam* but there
is no denying the enormity of their
impact, both in terms of international
projection and their effect domestically.
Not least to Montjuïc which was the
main focus of events, from the
spectacular opening ceremony in the
stadium to its jubilant closure. It had to
cope with hordes of people and millions
of television viewers, so it had to work

well and look good. A series of escalators was constructed to help move people around and the area around the stadium was landscaped, modern sculptures introduced, the space-age Palau Sant Jordi built by Isozaki, the sports university by Bofill and the striking Calatrava communications tower, as well as swimming pools and athletics tracks. It all looked very sleek, and still does. Sports enthusiasts can visit the stadium and see the exhibition on the event in the Galeria Olímpica behind.

Galeria Olímpica. Open: Tue–Sat 10am–1pm, 4–6pm, Sun 10am–2pm.

Cultural centre

The hill has been associated with cultural events for many years. Apart from the prized art collection in the Palau Nacional, there is the world-class Fundació Joan Miró and the new Caixa Forum, while architects from around the world flock to the Mies van der Rohe pavilion (*for all these see pp98–101*). In addition there are some good museums.

Museu d'Arqueologia de Catalunya, Passeig Santa Madrona 39–41.
Open: Tue–Sat 9.30am–7pm,
Sun 10am–2.30pm.
Museu Etnològic, Passeig Santa Madrona.
Open: Tue–Sun 10am–2pm.

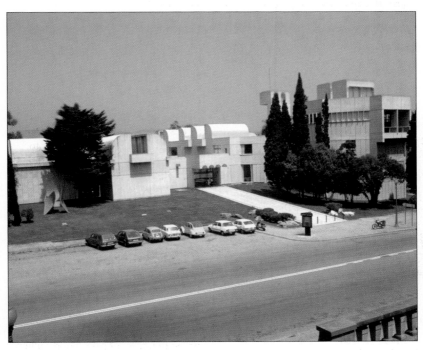

A visit to the Fundació Joan Miró is a must

Montjuïc also has a strong theatrical tradition. Plays and concerts held in the 'Greek' amphitheatre, also built for 1929, are a highlight of the annual Grec Festival, a summer festival of theatre, dance, music that runs from late June until early August. It is a magical setting on a hot summer night. Just at the foot of the hill on Carrer Lleida is 'Theatre Town', a complex of theatres which aims to provide a range of performances, from studio workshops to large-scale productions. The Teatre Lliure is now based here.

Castell de Montjuïc

At the summit is the Montjuïc castle which can be reached by cable car from the funicular terminus on Avinguda Miramar. This sturdy castle dates from the 17th century, though after being attacked by Bourbon troops it had to be rebuilt in the late 18th century. A tragic part of Catalonia's history took place here in 1940, when General Lluís Companys, president of the Generalitat, was executed by Franco's troops. It marked the beginning of the dark period of nearly 40 years of dictatorship. The castle houses a military museum with antique weapons, notably an 18th-century collection from Ripoll, uniforms and miniature soldiers.

Open: Tue–Sun 9.30am–5.30pm, Mar–Oct until 8pm.

The Museu Nacional d'Art de Catalunya (MNAC) has a wonderful Romanesque art collection

Wherever you are on Montjuïc there is a panoramic view

New plans

The latest phase in the development of this city hill is the Council's plan to encourage its use, claiming that few capitals can boast such an asset. New bus routes will make it easier to reach the hill, and once there new parts are being opened for walking or exploration, like the Camí del Mar. This is an attractive footpath that runs from just beneath the castle along the sea side of the hill, giving panoramic views of the busy working port. The old funfair has been landscaped and opened as the Joan Brossa Gardens, in memory of the charismatic poet/artist whose poetic sculptures can be seen all over the city. It has been planted with 'wild' flowers and has imaginative creative games for children. The Botanical Gardens opened a few years ago are now getting established and worth visiting and new footpaths are being developed. The aim is to offer a day out in the fresh air combining culture, sport and nature.

THE M CARD

The M Card is part of the new scheme to promote Montjuïc. It is a day pass which for a mere €20 opens up the hillside to you, from the Miró Foundation to the Picornell Olympic swimming pool. It allows you free admission to all the museums, events in the Caixa Forum, and the Poble Espanyol (the Spanish Village). You can travel around by cable car or tourist train, and at weekends you can use bicycles provided, all for free. After an exhausting day on the hill you can then use the pass for the theatre, either the Teatre Lliure or Mercat de Flors, if tickets are not sold out.

The M Card can be bought at any of the collaborating entities, the Tourist Office or through www.servicaixa.com. Cost: €20 for the day, €10 for children aged 6–12.

When enjoying the tangy air, delicious seafood and sunshine of Barcelona's waterfront, even long-time residents find it hard to remember that little more than a decade ago all this was a wasteland of derelict factories, warehouses and railway tracks. Barcelona is what it is today thanks to the Olympic Games of 1992. The Games brought far more than the promotion of Barcelona as a cosmopolitan capital, and far more than the stylish new residential neighbourhood of the Olympic Village and flagship sports facilities.

What the 1992 Olympics made possible was quite simply the revival of the entire city. Barcelona's determined bid to host them was a key element in the far-reaching municipal policy implemented after the first democratic elections of 1979. Staging the games was the key piece in a master plan to channel hard-earned money back into Barcelona for the benefit of its citizens.

During General Franco's dictatorship, with its *laissez-faire* economic policy and fierce repression of the Catalan identity, hard-working industrialised Barcelona and its metropolitan belt continued to be the economic powerhouse of Spain, and immigrants from the impoverished south poured in. Chronically underfunded, Barcelona became one of the world's most densely populated cities. Cheap housing was thrown up without a thought to infrastructure or amenities. Barcelona was choking to death.

Nothing less than total regeneration was the aim of the socialists who won the City Council in 1979. They initiated a new forward-looking urban policy, putting people and quality of life before profit. Subsidies were offered for restoring façades, green spaces were recovered, public amenities built. The hosting of the Olympic Games provided the ideal framework, the perfect way to obtain financing for the ambitious project that encompassed the whole city and its environs.

Radical improvement of the road system included the desperately needed ring road (Les Rondes) and expressway (Túnels de Vallvidrera) to the towns on the other side of Collserola. The airport was enlarged and innumerable buildings renovated. The waterfront and beaches were rescued and redeveloped. New buildings included the twin skyscrapers forming the gateway to the Olympic Port, Norman Foster's communications tower on Collserola and Calatrava's on Montjuïc, Isozaki's Palau Sant Jordi... the list goes on. During the dusty years of demolition and construction, the Council repeatedly promised disrupted citizens that it was the Barcelona of the future that was being built. Since the Games, the socialists have continued to hold the Council and to execute the development policy. That Barcelona is now a number-one destination has clearly proved them right.

Opposite: The Olympic Stadium
Above: A detail of the Palau Sant Jordi
Below: Diving events were impressive with a backdrop of the city

The Spanish Village on Montjuïc is one of the city's most popular sites, attracting 1.5 million visitors a year, most of them Spanish. This kitsch collection of fake buildings from different parts of the country has worn the passage of time with some dignity. Renovations in the late 1980s created within its walls one of the trendiest bars in the city and as it passes its 75th anniversary its owners see it becoming a centre of cultural and artisanal excellence.

The village was among many great fakes created for the 1929 World Exhibition on Montjuïc that included Venetian towers, Renaissance palaces and a Greek Theatre. It has around 120 houses, each from a different part of Spain. The architects, Francesc Folguera and Ramon Reventós, aided by the critic Miguel Utrillo and the artist Javier Nogués, had travelled the country to research their project, looking at typical houses built between the 11th and 20th centuries. The result is a surprisingly harmonious community centred on an arcaded Plaça Major, with pavement cafés and a town hall from Valderrobles in Teruel. There are balconies from the Basque country, stone houses from Extramadura, courtyards from Seville and a selection of buildings from the pilgrims' route to Santiago de Compostella. Today, people who are restoring old houses even come to carry out their research.

The crafts of the nation were also shown in the original exhibition, and later there were two museums showing popular traditions, crafts and the graphic arts. The artisan workshops have been revived and there are nearly 40 of them engaged in printing, glass blowing and other traditional activities. The village, which is privately owned, has ambitions to become an 'artisanal reference centre'. There are also three art schools and several businesses based in the buildings.

Souvenir shops, a bank and tourist information office add to the theme-park feel, but Barcelonans make it their entertainment place of choice in the evenings and at weekends when flamenco, audiovisual programmes and other shows are regularly staged. There are also some 17 restaurants to choose from and a number of bars.

The whole complex is wrapped around by a copy of the 11th-century walls of Àvila, in central Spain, with its Puerto de San Vicente forming the entrance. Inside one of the gate's towers is the Torres de Àvila, a bar created in 1990 by the architect Alfredo Arribas and the designer Javier Mariscal, which for a while was the trendiest place in town. With myriad rooms and a roof terrace giving spectacular views over the city, it is worth checking out. Today the venue is a dance club.

Just outside the walls are a new sculpture garden and a replica monastery from the province of Girona. *Marqués de Comillas, Parc de Montjuïc. Tel: 93 325 78 66. www.poble-espanyol.com. Open: Mon 9am–8pm,*

Tue–Thur 9am–2am, Fri–Sat 9am–4am, Sun 9am–midnight. Admission charge. Metro: Espanya. Bus: 13 or 50.

Above: Artworks are on sale in the village centred on Plaça Major (opposite)
Below: Santiago Cathedral in miniature

Walk: Montjuïc

The best way to visit the key sites on Montjuïc hill is on foot, using the escalators for the steep bits. Currently undergoing a revival, more gardens and green spaces are becoming accessible to the public, and a new walkway has opened near the castle, overlooking the port and the Mediterranean beyond. For the adventurous and energetic there are infinite walks on this hill, one of Barcelona's landmarks.

Allow half a day.

Start in Plaça Espanya, easily reached by metro lines 1 or 3.

1 Plaça Espanya

This busy roundabout is a gateway out of Barcelona, funnelling traffic south while the incoming traffic roars underneath it, and a strategic point for visitors to Montjuïc and the two million visitors a year that flood into the Fira de Barcelona, the Trade Fair site along Avinguda Reina Maria Cristina. Its central statue was erected for the 1929 Universal Exposition. Entitled 'Spain', it was designed by Jujol, one of Gaudí's collaborators, though his usual original *modernista* style was evidently repressed, probably by demands from central government in Madrid who were very influential in the Exposition. The former bullring Las Arenas, dating from 1900, is going the way of many old characters in this rapidly developing city, and is about to be reborn as a Richard Rodgers commercial centre. The twin 'Venetian' towers were the main entrance to the 1929 Exposition.

2 Font Màgica

On the first esplanade is the much-loved Magic Fountain. This was designed by

Carlos Buigas in 1929, and after recent restoration is still plying away with its colourful show from Thursday to Sunday evenings between June and September (8pm–midnight).

3 Caixa Forum

At this stage take an optional but recommended detour a short way along the Avinguda Marquès de Comillas to

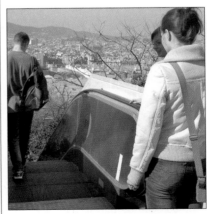

Escalators make it easier to get around the hill

Escalator

the magnificent Caixa Forum, the new cultural centre of the affluent 'La Caixa' Foundation. Also known as the Casaramona, it was an award-winning textile factory designed in 1911 by Puig i Cadafalch. It has a stunning new glass entrance designed by Isozaki leading into a huge space on several levels offering concerts, exhibitions and lectures, along with a media library open to the public, and the Foundation's vast contemporary art collection. The building alone is worth visiting, a fine example of Catalan *modernista* industrial architecture.
Av Marquès de Comillas 6–8. Tel: 902 22 30 40. www.fundacio.lacaixa.es. Open: Tue–Sun 10am–8pm. Closed: Mon. Free

admission. Check local listings for arts and music festivals held here.

4 Pavelló Mies van der Rohe

Another extraordinary architectural gem, once described as a building 'which will one day be remembered as the most beautiful of those built throughout the 20th century'. Designed by Mies van der Rohe as the German pavilion for the 1929 Exposition it seems totally modern in stark contrast with the other elaborate buildings built on the hill at the same time. Dismantled after the Exposition, it was rebuilt in the 1980s by a group of Barcelona architects, utterly faithful to the original.
Open: daily 10am–8pm. Admission

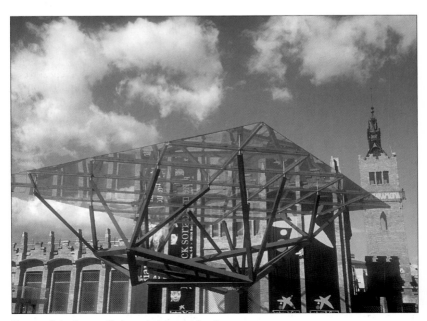

The new Caixa Forum offering entertainment for all

charge. Return to Magic Fountain and ride the escalators up the hill past more 1929 pavilions now used for trade fairs.

5 Palau Nacional

This monumental building that dominates Montjuïc has been the home of the Museu Nacional d'Art de Catalunya (otherwise known as the MNAC) since 1934. Its highly prized collection of Catalan Romanesque art, much of it carefully rescued from village churches in the Pyrenees, is breathtakingly beautiful. It also has a Gothic collection, some Renaissance and Baroque pieces, and holds interesting temporary exhibitions.
Mirador Palau Nacional 6–10. Tel: 936 22 03 75. www.mnac.es. Open: Tue–Sat 10am–7pm, Sun 10am–2.30pm. Admission charge.

6 Olympic stadium and complex

More escalators behind the Palau Nacional lead up to Avinguda de l'Estadi. Here the mountain opens up to the south-east and the Olympic complex spreads over it. The high-tech Palau Sant Jordi, another Isozaki piece, was used for the indoor events and now divides its time between mega rock concerts and sundry sports championships. The Olympic stadium was adapted from the original 1929 stadium to accommodate 55,000 spectators.
Open: daily 10am–8pm, in winter until 6pm.

7 Fundació Joan Miró

A short walk along the road is one of the largest collections in the world of Miró's art, housed in a spectacular museum designed by his close friend Josep Lluís Sert. The Mediterranean light that floods into the building shows Miró's work at its best. The restaurant has an attractive courtyard which is very pleasant for lunch.
Av Miramar 1. Tel: 934 43 94 70. www.bcn.fjmiro.es. Open: Tue–Sat 10am–7pm, Thur 10am–9.30pm, Sun 10am–2.30pm. Closed: Mon. Admission charge.

8 Torre Calatrava

Another landmark, this communication tower was designed by Valencian architect Santiago Calatrava for the 1992 Olympics. It is one of the symbols of the new Barcelona that has been projected to the world during and since the Games.

9 Poble Espanyol

Another legacy of the 1929 Exposition, the Spanish Village was built to show the different regional architectures of Spain along with various arts and crafts (*see pp96–7*). Something of a pastiche, it still draws the crowds and is a big hit with children. In its latest lease of life it has become a popular nightlife venue, especially for late-night dancing in summer. Some of the concerts during the Grec Summer Festival are held in its Plaza Mayor.
From the Poble Espanyol you can head back past the Olympic stadium and the Fundació Joan Miró, from where you can catch the funicular to metro line 3, just along Avinguda Miramar. Or you can continue along the Avinguda Marquès de Comillas back to the Magic Fountain.

Parc de la Ciutadella

The city's largest park blossomed from one of the most hated symbols of the power of Madrid – a fortress built by the conquering Bourbons. For two centuries it was a gloomy, forbidding place and when it finally came down nobody mourned its passing. From then on everyone could enjoy a new pleasure garden – and a World Fair that celebrated a new era.

Fontseré's formal gardens

After the besieged city of Barcelona was finally defeated by Felipe V's Franco-Spanish troops in 1714, a fortress was built as barracks for 8,000 troops to make sure that disagreements with the capital never led to warfare again. It was just one of many draconian measures introduced by the new Bourbon ruler, including the banning of the Catalan language and the closing of the city's university.

Oppressive prison

Forty streets and more than 1,200 houses were demolished to make way for the star-shaped fortress designed by Prosper Verboom, and the inhabitants were only belatedly given new housing in Barceloneta (*see pp32–3*). In fact the building was never used as a barracks, but it became a prison, used by Napoleon's troops when they invaded and afterwards for liberals opposed

A playground in the park, which attracts families with its pleasant gardens and boating lake

Giraffes in the city zoo, which occupies the southern part of the park

to the government in Madrid. It was therefore with enormous zeal that the place was torn down in 1869 when the country's liberal leader General Prim, himself a Catalan, gave the lands to the city to turn into a public park. In gratitude the city erected an equestrian statue of him in its centre.

Exhibition space

The main architect for the park was Josep Fontseré i Mestres who, with a team of designers that included a fledgling Gaudí, set about producing lawns, lakes, plots, parterres, and the Cascada, a fountain with Neptune, sea horses and a grotto. The grand plan all came together in time for the Universal Exhibiton of 1888, when early *modernista* buildings were added to the 19th-century grandeur. The exhibition was open for just 6 months, attracting around 6,000 people a day. They came

to ride in a hot air balloon and gape at such novelties as a giant sculpture of Mozarella cheese as well as to visit palaces devoted to science, agriculture and the arts. When the exhibition closed most of the buildings were pulled down.

Verboom's arsenal, meanwhile, had not been destroyed but remodelled, and it is now the seat of the Catalan parliament and home to the Museu d'Art de Catalunya. Outside this building in Plaça de Armes, laid out by the French landscape gardener Jean Forestier, is an elegant sculpture by Josep Limona in the middle of a pond. But the park's best loved sculpture stands outside the zoo, which arrived at the turn of the century. The fashionable *Dama del Paraigua* (*Woman with an Umbrella*) by Roig i Soler, holds out her hand as rain cascades down over her umbrella. She has become a charming mascot of the city.

Walk: Parc de la Ciutadella

There is something for everyone in this tranquil leisure ground that is enjoyed by Barcelonans all the year round. Parakeets escaped from the Rambla squawk in its trees and buggies are pushed around its broadwalk among flowerbeds and plantations. The lake attracts idle rowers, there are benches for the weary and lawns for lovers to lie on. Add a zoo and a museum or two, and the picture of a leisurely outing is complete.

Allow three hours or more, depending on how much diverts your attention.

Start at the Arc de Triomf (Metro line 1). Exit on to Carrer de Wellington for the Ciutadella–Villa Olímpica metro (line 4).

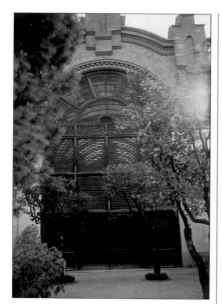

The Umbracle is full of tropical plants

1 Arc de Triomf

Based on Napoleon's triumphal arch in Paris, this one was erected as the entrance to the 1888 Universal Exhibition that filled the park. Still in an imposing position at the end of the long avenue of Passeig Sant Joan and near the law courts and the temporary Mercat de Santa Caterina, the red-brick and white-marble building in a *mudéjar* style remains impressive. It was designed by Josep Vilaseca i Casanovas with a frieze by Josep Reynés depicting Barcelona welcoming visitors to the city.

2 Museu de Zoòlogia

The zoological museum is housed in the Castell dels Tres Dragons ('Castle of the Three Dragons'), which was designed by Domènech i Montaner as the café-restaurant for the Universal Exhibition. Contemporary exhibitions are held here to counter the musty feel of an old-fashioned collection of molluscs, insects and invertebrates. The nearby **Museu de Geologia**, with a collection of minerals, fossils and rocks and an explanation of the region's substrata, was the city's first museum, built in 1878, and it has an equally 19th-century feel. *Passeig de Picasso. Tel: 933 19 69 12. Open: Tue–Sun 10am–2pm. Admission charge; combined tickets for both museums available.*

3 Hivernacle

Between the two museums is a delightful hothouse filled with tropical plants. There is a bar and a good restaurant inside. It stays open late and has jazz and concert evenings, which are well worth looking out for. It is complemented on the other side of the Museu de Geologia by the **Umbracle**, another hothouse of wood, brick and elegant iron pillars designed by Fontseré, the park's principal architect. *Passeig de Picasso. Tel: 934 24 38 09.*

4 Museu d'Art Modern

The museum shares a building with the Parlament de Catalunya and contains work by all the important 19th- and 20th-century Catalan artists who do not have museums of their own. Essentially these are the works of *modernista* and *noucentisme* artists, such as Mir, Nonell, Casas and Rusiñol, but there are also some beautiful

A mammoth outing for a child in the zoo

pieces of furniture by Gaudí and others, which altogether add up to a vital element in understanding the modern city's cultural heritage.

Parc de la Ciutadella, Metro: line 1 (Arc de Triomf) and line 4 (Barceloneta). Tel: 933 19 5728. www.mnac.es. Open: Tue–Sat 10am–7pm, Sun & holidays 10am–2.30pm. Closed: Mon. Admission charge.

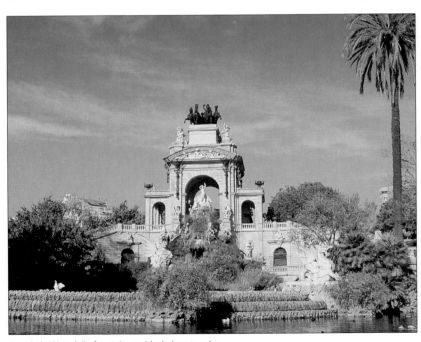

Parc de la Ciutadella fountain, an ideal place to relax

5 Parc Zoològic

The city zoo is a favourite attraction and its star performer for many years has been Snowflake, an Albino gorilla with attitude. The zoo has an enlightened programme of conservation and collaborates on a number of international and European programmes for breeding and preserving species threatened with extinction. There is a plan to move the zoo further up the coast to the Riva Besós, and turn the site into a further recreation area of the park. *Parc de la Ciutadella. Tel: 932 25 67 80. www.zoobarcelona.com. Open: 10am–5pm; May–Aug 9.30am–7.30pm. Admission charge.*

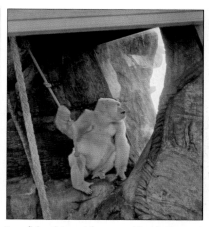

Snowflake, the most famous resident in the zoo

The attractive Hivernacle is a pleasant spot for a drink

Park Güell

The Park Güell is a supreme example of Gaudí's bold genius, built at a time when the use of local rustic stone and indigenous plants and the recycling of stone and ceramics were seen as utterly eccentric. Originally intended to be a garden city, probably inspired by models of the time that emerged as a reaction to the filthy, ugly cities of the industrial revolution, it integrates architecture and nature in a whole of unique loveliness.

One of 84 Doric columns at Park Güell

In the late 19th century the cultured aristocrat Eusebi Güell bought a property on a bare hillside above Gràcia and commissioned Gaudí, with whom he shared both aesthetic and nationalist ideas, to carry out the project. The area intended for communal amenities was practically the only part built, since the project foundered through lack of interest from the conventional Eixample-dwelling bourgeoisie, with only a couple of plots sold. After Güell's death in 1918, his heirs sold the property to the City Council for it to be turned into a public park. It was declared a UNESCO World Heritage Site in 1984 and has since been restored.

The 'fairy-tale' architecture and flowing forms that are almost synonymous with Gaudí are underpinned by meticulous calculation of every single technical detail. The estate

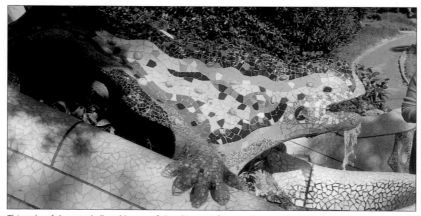

This colourful, ceramic lizard is one of Gaudí's most famous visual symbols

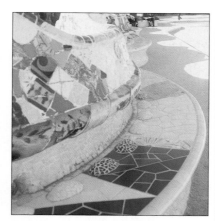

Trencadís work on the undulating beach

was divided into triangular lots linked by paths and viaducts winding round the hill. The three viaducts formed a brick service structure which Gaudí then clad in local stone and endowed with sculptural value. The result is a merging of nature and stone, with tunnels, bridges and lookouts to surprise the visitor. While the lower viaduct is sober, the upper ones grow increasingly ornamented, with double colonnades, a wave-like inner profile, and a texture resembling molten wax. The top viaduct is twisting and heavy, with chubby columns and sculpted jardinières. The ensemble was planned to accommodate climbing and hanging plants.

While the architectural elements of the park clearly get the most attention, it also reveals Gaudí as an ecologist before his time. The original vegetation was very sparse, and he planned a Mediterranean wood, with native species that would proliferate spontaneously. Thick pine groves and existing trees were reinforced by various plantations and ornamental species with spectacular blossoms. The rest is now a dense wood, carpeted with shrubs and crossed by dirt paths and stone stairways. The park contains several listed trees, including an ancient carob growing in the middle of the path on the central viaduct. Gaudí bumped into the tree as the work progressed and refused to have it cut down. The wood is also home to more than 60 species of bird, some permanent residents, others migratory.

At one end of the park (going left from the entrance), where the church was to be built, Gaudí made a stone promontory with a rather primitive aspect, with three crosses at its summit, reached by a rough flight of steps. At the back of the park on the other side of the hill is the traditional fountain of Sant Salvador, remodelled in 1984. The spacious plaza has a children's playground and a fabulous view over the city.

One of the gatehouses to the park

Antoní Gaudí i Cornet

With fluid lines, decorative ironwork and soaring flights of fancy, the architecture of Antoní Gaudí i Cornet is a symbol of Barcelona. Devoted both to the church and to Catalan nationalism, he was a master mason, painter and sculptor who relied on his own hands and eyes rather than on measurements and calculations. His organic buildings are a heady mix of styles, a peculiar Catalan neo-Gothic.

Gaudí was born in 1852, and while attending Barcelona's School of Architecture he worked in creating the new Parc de la Ciutadella. After graduating, his first and only municipal commission was for street lamps in the Plaça Reial, which are still in place.

After two important building projects, Casa Vicens in Barcelona and El Capricho

in northern Spain, Gaudí had his first commission from his most generous patron, the industrialist Count Eusebi Güell. The commission was for what is now known as the Güell Pavilion, on the count's farm estate in Pedralbes. A typical Catalan polymath, Güell was also a politician and supporter of the arts. His home in Carrer Nou de la Rambla was always full of social gatherings and in the 1880s Gaudí designed a new extension. The resulting Palau Güell (*see p89*), Gaudí's only building in the old town, was a gloomy Gothic masterpiece and Güell declared that he liked it less and less the higher it grew. Famously, he never ventured on to its elaborate roof to see its glazed and decorated chimneys.

But he liked it enough to give Gaudí another major commission, Park Güell (*see pp108–9*). It was to be a model community with 60 houses but only two were completed, one of which Gaudí made his home – it is now the Casa-Museu Gaudí. And when Güell installed a new textile plant at Santa Coloma, 17km (11 miles) west of Barcelona, he asked Gaudí to build a church, but the death of the wealthy patron in 1918 left it incomplete.

Bellesguard, a severe Gothic mansion beneath Tibidabo (*Carrer de Bellesguard 16–20*), was completed in 1902, and his most restrained building, the Casa Calvet (*Carrer de Casp 48*) was finished two years later. This was followed by Casa Batlló in Passeig de Gràcia and his final commission, Casa Milà, known as La Pedrera (*see p68*). These two Eixample showcases both have extraordinary Gaudí interiors.

After completing La Pedrera in 1910, unwashed and unpaid, Gaudí devoted

himself entirely to the Sagrada Família (*see pp114–15*), a project he had already been involved with for 17 years. He ended his days here as a recluse, living in a hut on the site, and when he was run down by a tram in Gran Via in 1926 and taken to hospital, he remained unrecognised for two days, dying shortly afterwards. The building had been the climax of his life's labour and with it he ensured that his name would forever be linked with the city.

Left top: La Pedrera, Gaudí's apartment block on Passeig de Gràcia
Left and opposite: towers and colonnades in Park Güell
Above: Casa Batlló in Passeig de Gràcia

Walk: Park Güell

In Gaudí's Park Güell, all the architectural elements blend
effortlessly with nature. Barcelona's famous visual symbols
such as the 'gingerbread house', the mosaic lizard and the
monumental plaza combine with fabulous views over the
city and quieter stretches of Mediterranean wood to make
this a unique, unmissable wonder.

Allow 3 hours.

*The walk begins at the main entrance to the park on Carrer
Olot, reached by bus 24 or metro (line 3) to Lesseps.*

1 Entrance

The gate, by Gaudí, originally
belonged to the Casa Vicens
and was put here in 1965.
With their curved lines and
mosaic ceramic roofs, the
two pavilions flanking the
entrance immediately take
us into a fairy-tale world. In
fact everything in the park is
filled with symbolic elements
that are difficult to interpret.
One of these buildings was
designed as living quarters
for the janitors of the garden
city and the other for visitor
reception and telephones.

2 Staircase

The monumental staircase
was conceived as the formal
entrance to the communal
areas of the garden city, but
its scale is softened by the
ornamentation, including
the famous water-spitting
lizard or dragon, and the

vegetation. It is difficult to know what mythical world Gaudí had in his head, but he still thought of every practical detail: the vault to the right of the staircase was to provide shelter on rainy days.

3 Sala Hipòstila and Plaça de la Natura

The Hypostyle Hall was originally intended as the market place and the spectacular plaza above it as the main communal space for cultural activities. The hall has 86 columns 6.16m (22ft) tall; the outer ones are inclined and act as buttresses. Gaudí's touch is visible in their irregular arrangement. Some of the columns enclose gutters which drain rainwater from the plaza into an underground tank, the lizard being the overflow pipe. The columns partly hold up the plaza, a real amphitheatre overlooking the city, edged by the famous undulating bench decorated with *trencadís* (pieces of ceramic). The whole ensemble has been painstakingly restored.

The famous serpentine bench was mostly the work of Jujol

4 Viaducte de la Bugadera

The natural, organic forms of the viaducts conceal meticulous calculations of differing inclines for pedestrians and carriages. The 3km (2 miles) of paths follow a formal logic which Gaudí breaks now and then with playful details, such as the lone figure of a washerwoman. The original figure held a washboard and was later reconstructed.

Follow the long route around the park via the Turó de les Menes with its three crosses – a steep but worthwhile climb.

5 Casa-Museu Gaudí

This building, by Francesc Berenguer, was the showhouse. Gaudí bought it with his meagre savings and lived in it with his father and niece until he went to live on-site at the Sagrada Família. In his will he stipulated that the house be sold and the proceeds go to the building of that church. It was bought by the Friends of Gaudí in 1963 to be turned into a museum. In it one can see furniture and rooms of the period, reproductions of Gaudí pieces and a small garden with a pergola.

Sagrada Família

One of the world's most extraordinary churches, the Sagrada Família has been more or less a building site for more than a century. Gaudí's lofty plans have been scaled back considerably in an effort to see it completed. But it still has a long way to go.

Christ and a pillar, Sagrada Família

The idea for a new church in Barcelona came from a local bookseller, Josep Bocabella, who had founded a religious society devoted to St Joseph and a better understanding between workers and employers. The site was purchased and the architect hired, but Francesc de

Paula Villar i Lozano, who produced a design based on a Gothic cathedral, had completed only a small section of the crypt when he fell out with Bocabella in 1883, a year after work began. Antoni Gaudí, then 31, was asked to take over.

Grand plans

Gaudí's plans for the Temple Expiatori de la Sagrada Família (The Holy Family Church of the Atonement) grew by the day. He conceived a huge building 60m (197ft) wide at the transept with a nave 90m (295ft) long and an external ambulatory or cloister that would entirely surround the building. The nave would look like a forest of stone pillars and the stone seats designed to seat 1,300 were to be placed close together to prevent people crossing their legs. By the time of his death in 1926 only the crypt, the apse, one tower and the beautifully sculpted Nativity façade – the one in all the postcards – had been completed. The centre of the building had become a stonemasons' quarry and though he left no detailed plans he made it clear that those who came after him should have the freedom to do what they thought best for the building.

Work on the church stopped during the Civil War, when models were broken

The towers with mosaics and tinkling bells

and drawings destroyed. It resumed in 1952, getting a boost in the 1980s when the Passion façade was created with sculptures by Josep Maria Subirachs, an avowed atheist. They seem at odds with Gaudí's Nativity figures, which are being continued by a Japanese sculptor, Etsuro Sotoo. Bright Venetian mosaics have been added to the top of the playful tinkling bell towers and to avoid the 400 steps in the spiral staircases a lift rises to the giddy heights of the towers where there are bird's-eye views of the church and the city. In the crypt, where Gaudí is buried, there is a museum and an altar for services.

Future work

The south façade, designed to be the main entrance to the building, and the entire nave are yet to be built. It is still envisaged that a central spire, much taller than the city cathedral's, will be surrounded by four large towers representing the evangelists. The weight of all this additional stonework will require a foundation of thousands of tons of concrete.

The debate about whether it is actually worth finishing the workers' church or if it is better just to leave it as a monument to its creator has gone on since Gaudí's death. In the meantime the building creeps ever heavenward. *Carrer de Mallorca 401. Tel: 934 55 02 47. www.sagradafamilia.org. Open: Oct–Mar 9am–6pm, Apr–Sept 9am–8pm. Admission charge. Metro: Sagrada Família (lines 2 and 5). Bus: 19, 33, 34, 43, 44, 50, 51.*

Inside, the nave is growing a forest of irregular pillars. Gaudí never thought in straight lines

Walk: around Sagrada Família

Too many visitors flock to the Sagrada Família by Metro, bus or taxi, take the obligatory tour and return exhausted to their hotels, missing some of the other *modernista* sites in the vicinity. This walk covers a few of these designed by contemporaries of Gaudí.

Allow 3 hours.

Take metro (line 5) to Hospital de Sant Pau or line 4 to Guinardó. The walk begins at the entrance to the hospital on Sant Antoni Maria Claret.

1 Hospital de Sant Pau

A hospital it is worth being sick for. When this quite magnificent complex was built in 1901 it was the most advanced hospital in Europe. Designed by Lluís Domènech i Montaner, it has separate pavilions set amongst gardens full of light and space. A subterranean labyrinth connects the pavilions. Visitors are free to wander around and enjoy the colourful tile-work and elaborate details which are the hallmark of this prolific architect.

2 Sagrada Família

From the hospital follow Avinguda Gaudí down until it joins the Nativity façade of Barcelona's most famous building. Take the opportunity to appreciate its exterior from all angles, but save the details and tower climbing for a separate visit (*see pp114–15*). Walk past the Gloria façade on Mallorca and glimpse the Passion façade sculpted by contemporary artist Subirachs. The park opposite often has outdoor markets which are well worth a visit.

3 Casa Macaya

Designed in 1901 by the third of Barcelona's most famous *modernista* architects, Josep Puig i Cadafalch. Originally a town house, it now belongs to the La Caixa Foundation and is temporarily being used by the foundation's excellent science museum. Be sure to wander in to see the magnificent courtyard with an exterior staircase.
Passeig Sant Joan 106.

4 Casa Terrades

This part of the Diagonal shows the Eixample at its most elegant, part of the so-called *Quadrat d'Or* or Golden Square where the most prized *modernista* buildings are found. Interesting hallways, jealously guarded by the *portero* or *portera* (caretaker), are a tempting appetiser to the world within. The Casa Terrades, also designed by Puig i Cadafalch in 1903, is no exception. Popularly known as the Casa de les Punxes (the 'house of spikes'), it is supposedly the only detached building

in the Eixample. It is not open to the public but there is plenty to feast on and fantasise about at street level in this fairy-tale building.
Av Diagonal 416–420.

5 Casa Asia

This is one of the most elaborate and decorative Puig i Cadafalch buildings. The Palau Baró de Quadras (1906) was for years the home of the Music Museum. Just reopened as 'Asia House', it holds exhibitions and other events always with an oriental theme and invites people to wander around its beautifully restored interior. Do not miss the rear which backs on to Rosselló.
Av Diagonal 373/Carrer Rosselló 279. www.casaasia.es. Open: Tue–Sat 10am–8pm, Sun 10am–2pm.

6 Casa Comalat

Another building which has to be seen from front and behind, so as not to miss a trick. Designed in 1911 by lesser-known architect Salvador Valeri.
Av Diagonal 442.

7 Casa Fuster

An elegant, quite subdued building, one of Domènech i Montaner's last pieces (1911). It wraps around the corner marking the end of Passeig de Gràcia, with spectacular views down the whole length of one of Barcelona's most elegant streets. It is being renovated as a hotel.
Passeig de Gràcia 132. Continue up Gran de Gràcia to explore the 'village' of Gràcia (see pp72–5) or return to the junction with Diagonal where there are metro and bus connections.

Sarrià and Pedralbes

Less than ten minutes by train from Plaça Catalunya, the former village of Sarrià is now part of the urban sprawl but still manages to retain a sense of village life with its pretty alleyways, small terraced houses with plants spilling over iron fences, and some ancient establishments. It provides an appealing contrast to the well-trodden tourist track and a good place for lunch or as a stepping-stone up to the Collserola park.

Relax in the village-like tranquillity of Sarrià

The main square, Plaça de Sarrià, is dominated by the church of Sant Vicenç. Nearby is the attractive covered market,

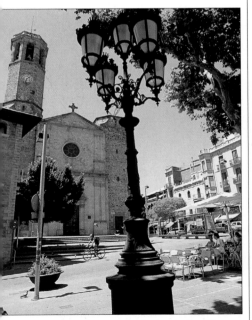

Sarrià's main square overlooked by Sant Vicenç church

dating from 1911, which perpetuates the sense of village life. Running down from the Plaça is the main street, Major de Sarrià, where a pause at Bar Tomàs (*Major de Sarrià 49*) is essential. People make the pilgrimage from all over the city for its famed *patatas bravas* (fried potatoes served with spicy sauce or mayonnaise). Alternatively plan a visit around lunchtime so you can eat *canalons* or one of the other home-made dishes in family-run Casa Joana. The side streets are worth exploring to find dimly-lit shops from another era and turn-of-the-century villas.

Beyond the nucleus, however, it becomes obvious that this is uptown and upmarket, and a desirable residential area. The official district is Sarrià–Sant Gervasi which comprises the even more desirable Pedralbes at one extreme and towards Tibidabo the Sant Gervasi area, with the highest concentration of private schools, hospitals and four-wheel-drives in Barcelona. In amongst the smart apartment blocks with manicured

Funicular travel makes Barcelona's steep hills more accessible

gardens are some interesting examples of *modernista* architecture, including two Gaudí buildings: the extraordinary convent Escola de les Teresianes (*Carrer Ganduxer*) which can be visited on Saturdays, and a private house Torre Bellesguard (*Carrer Bellesguard*).

The grass is definitely greener in Pedralbes, the air is much fresher and the density of population dramatically lower than in the Eixample or Ciutat Vella. It is favoured by expats, diplomats, and even royals. What it gains in air quality and reduced noise pollution, though, it lacks in the usual charms of a *barri* ('neighbourhood'). There is no corner shop here for last-minute shopping or gossip, nor the bustle of a local bar. However, it is home to one of the jewels in Barcelona's crown, the Monestir de Pedralbes, a haven of piece and tranquillity and well worth visiting (*see pp120–21*).

FUNICULAR DE VALLVIDRERA

Many of the houses on the hills above Sarrià were built in the late 19th or early 20th century for the middle-classes to *veranear*, or spend the hot summer months. The temperature is noticeably a few degrees cooler at these heights and it is less humid. Vallvidrera at the summit, today another 'urban village', was particularly popular. A funicular built in 1906 still provides the best possible means for getting up the hill from Peu de Funicular, the next station after Sarrià. Until 1998 the original wooden carriages were used, adding to the charm of the journey, though the modern vehicle is reassuringly efficient, and by special request will stop halfway up in Carretera de les Aigües. This is a rough road which circumnavigates the hill, ideal for exercise and lofty views of the city.

Though not in the centre of town, the Royal Monastery of Santa María de Pedralbes is worth the short journey. This beautiful religious enclave is one of the most important buildings of Catalan Gothic. An added pleasure are the sublime paintings and sculpture from the Thyssen-Bornemisza collection.

The monastery was founded in 1326 by Queen Elisenda de Montcada, the fourth wife of Jaume II. After his death the following year she took the order of St Clare and shut herself away here for the next 37 years. Some twenty nuns of the Order of St Clare still live near the monastery, in which they maintain an interest. They left the monastery in the early 1980s and the cells, refectory and infirmary they left behind still seem warm with life.

The monastery complex is approached through a stone portal that opens on to the gardens of the Plaça de Monestir. The church has a separate entrance beyond the monastery, and over its lintel are the arms of Elisenda, the Montcada family and the royal house of Barcelona. Queen Elisenda's tomb is set in the wall so it could be venerated both in the church and in the monastery, wearing her royal wedding dress on one side, a nun's habit the other.

The monastery is set around a cloister with a most elegant three-storey colonnade. The view of this cloister, with Cyprus and fruit trees and a perfect octagonal belfry, is a pinnacle of Catalan Gothic and is contemporary with the city's finest Gothic church, Santa María del Mar. Around the colonnaded cloisters are the bare cells of the nuns, with prie-dieux and small openings for food to be handed to them. The dispensary has various jars of medicines and potions, and the dining table in the refectory is laid and ready for food, which would have been grown from the vegetable gardens that can be glimpsed through the windows.

Just to the right as you arrive at the cloister is the Capella (chapel) de Sant Miguel, which has a beautiful mural of the life of Christ by the Ferrer Bassa, completed in 1346 for Francesca Saportella, abbess and niece of Queen Elisenda. Bassa had studied in Italy and this painting, which links Catalan Gothic to the Italian Renaissance, is the finest surviving Gothic painting in the city. To the left is the chapter house with a collection of relics and furniture from the monastery, including a model of the building.

At the far end of the cloister is the Queen's Hall and former dormitories, a large space now hung with more than 70 paintings and eight sculptures from the Thyssen-Bornemisza collection. These are mostly German, Dutch and Italian and include a lovely Fra Angelica of the Madonna of Humility, but there are also paintings by Velázquez and Zurbarán.

The paintings are part of the collection built up by two generations of the Thyssen-Bornemisza family of industrialists. Though domiciled in Switzerland, Hans Heinrich, the last Baron, donated the paintings to Spain, largely through the influence of his fifth wife, Carmen 'Tita' Cervera, a former Miss Spain. The largest part of the collection, which was permanently acquired by the state in 1993, is in the Villahermosa Palace in Madrid. *Carrer de Montevideo 14. Tel: 932 80 14 34. Open: 10am–2pm. Closed: Mon. Admission charge. Metro: Reina Elisenda.*

Opposite: Painting by Ferrer Bassa in the Church of Sant Miguel within the cloister of the Monastery of Pedralbes

Tibidabo and Collserola

The Collserola range of hills forms a backdrop to the city and a distinctive skyline with its high-tech communications tower and floodlit temple at the summit, Tibidabo. This is just the tip of its 8,000 hectares of parkland, Barcelona's hidden playground hardly used by most residents. Easily accessible, the area is well worth exploring for a breath of fresh air and spectacular views.

Norman Foster's communications tower

Carretera de les Aigües

This dirt track winds around the side of the hill on the city side for several kilometres, giving a bird's-eye view of the city. Over-populated with joggers and cyclists at weekends, it is ideal for exercise and getting the city into perspective during the week.
FGC to Peu del Funicular then funicular.
Press button to request stop at Carretera de les Aigües.

Parc de Collserola

The park stretching behind the hills

Lofty views are the compensation for climbing the Collserola hills is easily accessible from the centre of Barcelona and full of footpaths, picnic places, *merenderos* (shack-like restaurants where you can grill your own *botifarras*, Catalan sausages, or choose from the menu) and where the scent of the pine woods and the cooler air is a salvation in summer. During the week it is quiet enough to hear the birds singing and if you are lucky you may run into a family of *porc sanglars* (wild boar).

FGC train to Baixador de Vallvidrera, the first station after the tunnel through the hill, is only 13 minutes from Plaça Catalunya, and a good starting point.

Tibidabo

Legend has it that this was the hill where Christ was led by Satan to be tempted – *tibi dabo*, all this will I give you. Whether this be excess of Catalan pride or not, there is no denying that on a clear day the view over the city and the Mediterranean from its 512m (1680ft) peak is quite spectacular. The Parc d'Atraccions and church, Temple of Sagrat Cor, at the top are less interesting but the excursion is worthwhile. Rattle up to the base of the funicular in the Tramvia Blau, a pretty blue wooden tram still going strong after 100 years of service. It passes elegant *modernista* buildings, once the summer houses of the Catalan bourgeoisie and now divided into flats or offices, and stops in Plaça Doctor Andreu where the funicular completes the journey to the top.

As fairgrounds go, this is more attractive than most, thanks to its retro feel which along with the view appeals to bored parents. Children love it all,

especially the *montaña rusa* which seems to drop over the edge of the hillside. *Tel: 932 11 79 42. Open: Jul–Aug 12noon–1am; weekends only in winter; rest of year times vary. FGC: Av Tibidabo. Bus: 17.*

Torre de Collserola

Norman Foster's communications tower was designed for the 1992 Olympic Games, along with Santiago Calatrava's tower on Montjuïc. Often swathed in swirling mists, it is best to visit it on a clear day, and take the transparent lift to the observation platform 560m (1840ft) above sea level.

Open: Wed–Fri 11am–2.30pm, 3.30–8pm, Sat–Sun 11am–8pm. Admission charge. Bus 211 or walk from FGC Vallvidrera Superior.

All the fun of the fair in Tibidabo plus a view

Vila Olímpica

Built to accommodate the hundreds of athletes who swarmed into Barcelona in July 1992, the Olympic Village was a major undertaking which completely transformed an obsolete industrial zone – a vital element in the restructuring of the city.

Twin towers overlook the waterfront

Before the cynical gaze of neighbouring residents it was completed, albeit at the eleventh hour, and it was the scene of much festivity during the Games. Afterwards it seemed like a ghost town – but now, over ten years later, it has an established feel: the green spaces are lush, the children's parks are well used, and it is just another neighbourhood of Barcelona.

Urban art was a feature of '90s Barcelona

Its construction involved rerouting a railway line, a whole new sewerage system and the demolition of old factories. In today's bright sunlit streets, landscaped with gardens and looking over long stretches of golden sand, it is hard to imagine that until the late 1980s it was a drab no-go area where the beaches had become a dumping ground. A few strategic chimneys remain as a reminder of its industrial past.

The most distinctive elements in the new village are the twin towers forming a gateway to the Olympic Port and the sea (*see pp34–7*). Amidst the smart yachts and smooth motor cruisers in the marina is a municipal sailing school offering courses throughout the year and yachts for charter. The port is lined with restaurants of varying standards, fast food to fresh The main drag of the village itself is Avinguda Icària, with a 'hard park' designed by Enric Miralles running down the middle. A depressing shopping mall transports you to some unidentifiable city in the American mid-west, but it does include the best cinema complex in Barcelona, the Yelmo, where 15 screens show *v.o.* (original language) films. The surrounding blocks of apartments, however, are identifiably Barcelona. In keeping with the zeal to create a striking new city, architects from around the world as well as leading Spanish and Catalan architects were involved in its construction.

Some 200 new buildings were built, all with a different design. The most desirable are along Avinguda Salvador Espriu, where the flats have a sea view and the thundering Ronda Litoral (the ring road) is covered with gardens. The inland blocks have peaceful landscaped courtyards. Of particular architectural interest are the Eurocity buildings on the crossroads of Icària and Rosa Sensat by local architects Piñon and Vilaplana, and the Telefónica building on Icària by

Jaume Bach and Gabriel Mora. Property prices here are inaccessible to the average person, making it a privileged residential area. But it has taken off as a playground for Barcelonans with roller bladers, cyclists and skateboarders cruising along the front, swarms of promenading families and hordes of sun worshippers on the beaches, and a different crowd by night. The Vila Olímpica now merges with its neighbouring Poble Nou as an established part of the city, while the cranes have moved along to the end of the beaches to build the latest new district, Diagonal Mar.

The twin towers are the gateway between Olympic Village and Olympic Port

New Architecture

The combination of post-Franco energy and Barcelona winning its bid for the XXV Olympiad made for a high-octane mix in the 1980s and early '90s. Nowhere was this so clearly manifested as in the world of architecture. A lot of new building had to be achieved in record time, old buildings had to be renovated, and a huge urban renewal scheme had already begun.

Young architects were given the opportunity of a lifetime, and with due flair the challenge was taken up. International architects were also brought in. As well as the key Olympic buildings (see pp90–93 and 124–5), there are many other projects which merit attention.

One such project came out of Oriol Bohigas' new urban design department in the City Council. Disparagingly known as 'hard parks', they were more positively 'urban spaces' which in a city second only to Calcutta in density was a welcome prospect. Young architects came up with creative design solutions for making public spaces out of dark alleyways or abandoned land. One of the earliest examples was the Parc de l'Escorxador near Plaça Espanya, also known as the Parc de Joan Miró after his distinctive tall sculpture, *Woman and Bird*. Nearby is the famous Plaça dels Països Catalans by Viaplana, Piñon and Miralles who were to become star architects over the following years. Parc de la Creueta del Coll was built in a quarry, providing the neglected neighbourhood with a much-appreciated lake to swim in.

A second wave of architecture followed 1992. The Teatre Nacional, designed by Ricardo Bofill, was built near Plaça de les Glòries, followed a few years later by Rafael Moneo's concert hall, L'Auditori. Much of this second wave has been about urban renewal. Richard Meier's Contemporary Art Museum in the Raval was a vital piece in opening up this forsaken area. More recently the Rambla del Raval has opened, a new urban space letting light into a dark, dense neighbourhood.

The third wave has come with the new century, focusing on the Forum 2004 and the Diagonal Mar (*see pp58–9*). This is based on worthy principles of creating a new residential area and building a sustainable city, but the increasing demand for hotels and office space has provoked speculation on a large scale. Recent projects seem to be more geared towards commercialism than urban renewal. Bohigas was horrified by the World Trade Center, blocking the city's new view of the sea. The old bullring in Plaça Espanya is to become yet another commercial centre. It is to be hoped that some projects will straddle both camps, like the proposed hotel on the Rambla del Raval. Will it bring life and trade into a neglected area, or will it just alienate in an area short of public housing?

Opposite: Calatrava's Bac de Roda bridge
Above: Bach and Mora's striking building in the Olympic Village

Zona Universitaria

At the extreme end of Avinguda Diagonal, its furthest point from the sea, is one of the main entrances to Barcelona, bringing traffic from Madrid and Lleida. A confusion of slip-roads and junctions suddenly clears to reveal the long straight avenue plunging down towards the Eixample and the city centre. As the name suggests, this area is dominated by the university campus.

Faculty of Arts, Barcelona University

What to some appears to be a no-man's land scattered with high-rise buildings is to others the beginning of an open-air museum, where several generations of architects have left their show-pieces. Two of the latest buildings are the Hotel Rey Juan Carlos I and the neighbouring Palau de Congressos de Catalunya, both by local architect Carles Ferrater. The hotel accommodates the many delegates who now flood into Barcelona for

University buildings

conferences, and it is favoured by the Spanish royal family as well as world politicians for its capacity to be cordoned off. Its spacious gardens and lake were annexed from a beautiful old house, Torre Melina, which was demolished to make way for the hotel.

Bordering the other side of the avenue is the Parc de Cervantes, known for its roses, notably the off-white Barcelona rose. Opposite the park is an exclusive tennis club, the Reial Club Tennis Turó. Many of its members, like those of the nearby Polo Club, are typical residents of this area, a different world from downtown Barcelona.

The University of Barcelona began to expand into this area from its central headquarters in the 1950s, a plan which was accelerated by student unrest provoked by the Franco regime. The Faculty of Law, at No 684, was built in record time using prefabricated material to house the unruly young lawyers. It is considered the best example of the International Style in the city and stands out as a rarity, as modern architecture was being repressed by Madrid at the time.

Oriol Bohigas, instrumental architect in Olympic Barcelona, describes it as the city's 'first civilized modern public building' after the Civil War. In recent times the university site has expanded, with the new UPC (Polytechnic University of Catalonia) opening its southern campus here.

As the university faculties begin to merge with the domineering commercial buildings which continue to line the avenue as far as Plaça Francesc Macià there is a refreshing green space: the gardens of the royal palace, Palau de Pedralbes (*see pp130–31*), a welcoming haven of peace. From here the stream of students flows into the brisk march of

office workers, a perfect illustration of the Catalan work ethic. The mood only lightens when there is a Barça match in the Camp Nou stadium tucked in behind this part of the Diagonal. Then the crowds pour into the metro stations and towards their cars parked for miles around this area. Whether jubilant or depressed (in the dramatic way Barça supporters feel their team's losses) they are a colourful bunch. Lone pensioners, grandparents and grandchildren, fathers and daughters (and the boyfriend), foreign students, boisterous lads, the wide gamut of Barça devotees are a refreshing injection of life into this commercial and financial district.

Camp Nou, the home of FC Barcelona

Walk: Palau Reial de Pedralbes and Pabellons Güell

More of a meander than a walk, this gentle route visits a 20th-century royal palace, a couple of museums, some ornamental gardens and a lesser-known Gaudí site, all within an estate that used to belong to the Güell family. Allow 1–2 hours.

Take the metro (line 3) to Palau Reial, or try the luxury Tomb bus, an exclusive service that runs from Plaça Catalunya to Plaça Pius XII, with suede seats and elegant señoras. More expensive than the normal bus but much more comfortable, and cheaper than a taxi.

The Decorative Art museum housed in the Palau Reial in Pedralbes

Jardins del Palau Reial de Pedralbes

This public park in the grounds of the royal palace is peaceful and serene after the busy commercial Avinguda Diagonal. Its central part is laid out as an ornamental garden, and its gravel paths are a favourite for wedding photographs. The land used to be part of an estate owned by the Güell family, ceded by the son of Eusebi Güell for the construction of the palace. Wander off the beaten track and you may find the small fountain-cum-bench designed by Gaudí before 1884, which was rediscovered after 100 years of being overgrown with ivy.

Palau Reial de Pedralbes

The attractive palace is not as historic as it looks. It is the result of a conversion of one of the houses on the estate, Can Feliu, which with the agreement of the people of Barcelona was given to the king Alfonso XIII when he came to visit. It is occasionally used for state banquets but not open to the public, except for the wings housing the two museums.

Museu de Ceràmica and Museu de les Arts Decoratives

Located in the wings of the palace are these two small but interesting museums. The Ceramic Museum follows the history of Spanish pottery from the 11th century to the present, including some Miró and Picasso pieces. The Decorative Arts Museum looks at the design of everyday objects from medieval times until today. They both hold temporary exhibitions.

Open: Tue–Sat 10am–6pm, Sun 10am–3pm. Admission free on first Sun of month.

Leave the gardens and turn left down Diagonal to Plaça Pius XII, then left into the broad Avinguda Pedralbes, which goes up to the monastery (see pp120–21).

Facultat de Dret

On the corner is the Faculty of Law, one of the many university buildings in this upper part of Diagonal. Built in 1958, it is regarded as the best example of the International Style in Barcelona (*see pp128–9*).

Pabellons de la Finca Güell

One of the few Gaudí works you can see without the usual crush, being relatively far from the centre. This was the entrance to the Güell estate and consists of lodge houses and stables behind. The extraordinary gate is a sculpted dragon, an important mythical beast in Catalan culture. Not open to the public, but there are so many details to observe from the outside, right down to the delicate ceramic flecks in the brickwork. *Avinguda de Pedralbes 7, corner of George R Collins (street recently named after the American historian who promoted Gaudí's fame in the 1950s).*

Palau Reial is used for state banquets and has two museums

In May 1992, Ronald Koeman's penalty kick that netted the coveted European Cup for FC Barcelona for the first time in its history plunged all Catalonia into days of euphoric celebration. Since arch-rivals Real Madrid had already won the cup six times, nothing that Barcelona's celebrated Olympic Games were to bring would ever match that moment.

The slogan that has been repeated *ad nauseam* is true: '*Barça és més qu'un club*'. Barça is more than a club, more than a city football team: it is a national institution, a way of life. It draws supporters from the whole of Catalonia, and Catalan communities across the world have their *barcelonista* circles.

One of the oldest clubs in Europe, it was founded in 1899 and soon became well established. It always seemed, though, that the dice were heavily loaded in favour of Real Madrid, an organ of the central government. Barça's history is filled with incidents that show that this rivalry went far deeper than sport: it was a political issue. In one notorious episode, when Barcelona signed the brilliant player Kubala in 1951, their fortunes improved considerably and the team became so powerful that the Spanish government forced the removal of the equally brilliant DiStefano and dictated that he play for Real Madrid.

During the repressive Franco years, the team functioned as 'the army of Catalonia', for Barça was the only outlet for the collective expression of Catalan national identity. The Catalan flag was banned, and so the *blaugrana* (blue and garnet) flag took on huge significance. It was instrumental in integrating the huge numbers of immigrants from southern Spain and elsewhere, uniting them with the 'born and bred' Catalans in a common cause. Barça's vicissitudes are still followed with almost religious fervour, and victories are greeted with fireworks, partying crowds on the Rambla and honking horns.

Barça has strong roots in Catalan society. The club has over 100,000 members, most of whom have permanent seats, with membership passing from parent to child. Visitors can look around the fabulous Camp Nou Stadium and take in the FC Barcelona Museum (the city's second most visited one after the Picasso) which contains a blow-by-blow history of the club with audiovisuals, glittering trophies and an assortment of boots, shirts, photos, referees' whistles and other paraphernalia.

Barça also fields basketball, handball, ice hockey and roller hockey teams, with smaller though equally devoted followings. The winning of the European Cup by the basketball team in 2003 triggered ecstatic celebrations to equal any football triumphs.

Opposite page: Memorabilia in the 'Barça' museum
Above: A mecca for football fans everywhere

Museums

There are 68 museums in Barcelona, innumerable art galleries and several cultural centres run by local authorities and private organisations. Avoiding some of the more obscure, like the Museum of Horse-Drawn Hearses or the Museum of Dentistry, this list has been reduced to the most popular and best organised and includes the major cultural centres known for their high standard of exhibitions. Art galleries are all over town, but special concentrations of them are in Consell de Cent, near Passeig de Gràcia, and in the Old Town, the more avant-garde being in the Born and Raval neighbourhoods.

Many museum buildings are worth visiting in themselves

Caixa Forum

Fascinating *modernista* textile factory restored into 'la Caixa' Foundation's stimulating cultural centre, where their contemporary art collection, one of the largest in Europe, can be displayed. Music festivals, family activities, temporary exhibitions, conferences and media library are all available here. *Nits d'estiu* is a special programme of night-time events for summer evenings. (*See also pp98 and 100.*)
Av Marquès de Comillas 6–8. Tel: 902 22 30 40. www.fundacio.lacaixa.es. Open: Tue–Sun 10am–8pm. Closed: Mon. Free admission. Metro: Espanya.

Centre Cultural Caixa Catalunya (La Pedrera)

Gaudí's apartment block the Casa Milà, or La Pedrera, is owned by the Caixa Catalunya and used as their cultural centre. Apart from the Espai Gaudí, a useful exhibition of his work, and

El Pis, the show flat, there is space on the first floor with high quality temporary exhibitions free of charge. *Provença 261. Tel: 902 40 09 73. www.caixacatalunya.es. Open: daily 10am–8pm. Closed: Mon. Admission charge (to Espai and El Pis/roof terrace). Metro: Diagonal. FGC: Provença.*

Fundació Antoni Tàpies

Comprehensive collection of one of Catalonia's and Spain's greatest living artists, Antoni Tàpies, mostly donated by the artist himself. Shows the evolution of his work. *Aragó 255. Tel: 934 87 03 15. www.fundaciotapies.org. Open: Tue–Sun 10am–8pm. Closed: Mon. Admission charge. Metro: Passeig de Gràcia.*

Fundació Joan Miró

Large collection of Miró's work from 1914 to 1978, including paintings, sculptures, drawing and textiles. Also

houses the Mercury fountain designed by Alexander Calder for the Spanish Republican pavilion in the 1937 Paris Exhibition. Holds an annual festival of contemporary music.
Av Miramar 1. Tel: 934 43 94 70. www.bcn.fjmiro.es. Open: Tue–Sat 10am–7pm, Thur 10am–9.30pm, Sun 10am–2.30pm. Closed: Mon. Admission charge. Metro: Paral.lel + Funicular. Bus: 50, 55.

Fundació Thyssen Bornemisza

The Old Masters section of the collection Baron Thyssen Bornemisza gave to Spain is housed in the wonderful setting of the Monestir de Pedralbes (*see pp120–21*). It includes pieces by Fra Angelico, Tiziano, Zurbarán and Canaletto.
Baixada Monestir 9. Tel: 932 80 14 34. www.museothyssen.org. Open: Tue–Sun 10am–2pm. Closed: Mon. Admission charge. Metro: Maria Cristina. FGC: Reina Elisenda. Bus: 22, 63, 64.

Museu d'Art Contemporani de Barcelona (MACBA)

A striking building houses the contemporary art collection that is almost more about urban renewal programmes than art (*see p50*).
Plaça dels Angels 1. Tel: 934 12 08 10. www.macba.es. Open: 11am–7.30pm, Sat 10am–8pm, Sun 10am–3pm. Closed: Tue. Admission charge. Metro: Catalunya or Universitat. FGC: Catalunya.

Museu d'Art Modern (MNAC)

A pleasing collection from the 19th and early 20th centuries, covering the work of artists that were in the same circle as Picasso at the turn of the century. Note

the work of Casas, Nonell, Rusiñol. This collection is due to join the rest of the National Art Museum in the Palau Nacional on Montjuïc so check whether it has moved yet.
Parc de la Ciutadella. Tel: 933 19 57 28. Open: Tue–Sat 10am–7pm, Sun 10am–2.30pm. Closed Mon. Admission charge. Metro: Arc de Triomf or Barceloneta. Bus: 14, 42, 59, 64.

Museu de Cera

The wax museum near the end of La Rambla is amusing for children on a rainy day.
Pasatge Banca 5–7. Tel: 933 17 26 49. www.museocerabcn.com. Open: Mon–Fri 10am–1.30pm, 4pm–7.30pm; Sat–Sun 11am–2pm, 4.30pm–8.30pm. Daily until 10pm in summer. Admission charge. Metro: Drassanes. Bus: 14, 59, 64.

Museu de la Ciència Fundació la Caixa

Excellent science museum owned by la Caixa Foundation, with plenty of

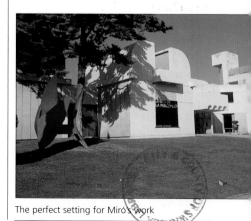

The perfect setting for Miró's work

A Tàpies sculpture crowns the *modernista* building that houses his work

hands-on activity for all ages. Fun and inspiring. Currently being extended on a major scale, it is bound to re-emerge as something well worth visiting.
Temporarily installed in Passeig Sant Joan 108. Tel: 932 12 60 50. www.fundacio.lacaixa.es. Check local listings to see if museum has returned home and for opening times etc.

Museu d'Història de Catalunya

The museum of Catalonia's history works as a generic history museum as well and is interesting for all the family. Try on a medieval knight's armour, build a Roman arch, there is plenty to do. Housed in a stylishly renovated warehouse on the harbour.
Plaça Pau Vila 3. Tel: 932 25 47 00. cultura.gencat.net/mhc. Open: Tue–Sat 10am–7pm, Sun 10am–2.30pm. Closed: Mon. Admission charge. Metro: Barceloneta. Bus: 14, 17, 59, 64.

Museu d'Història de la Ciutat

Fascinating insight into the history of Barcelona, including an underground visit to 4,000sq m (43,000sq ft) of archaeological remains beneath the square and the cathedral, from 1 BC to AD 9. You can also climb to the top of a 16th-century watchtower.
Plaça del Rei. Tel: 933 15 11 11. www.bcn.es/cultura. Open: Tue–Sat 10am–8pm, Sun 10am–3pm. Oct–May closed at lunchtime. Closed: Mon. Admission charge. Metro: Jaume I, Liceu or Catalunya. Bus: 16, 17, 40, 45.

Museu Futbol Club Barcelona President Nuñez

An essential for football fans this museum of Barça paraphernalia includes a spectacular view of the stadium, and a chance to skate on the ice-skating rink. (*See pp132–3.*)
Aristides Maillol 12–18. Enter through gates 7 or 9. Tel: 934 96 36 00. www.fcbarcelona.com. Open: Mon–Sat 10am–6.30pm, Sun 10am–2pm. Closed when a match is on. Admission charge. Metro: Collblanc. Bus: 15, 52, 53, 54.

Museu Marítim

The maritime museum has recently been refurbished to include a space for temporary exhibitions, and to show more of these impressive medieval shipyards (*see p54*). Part of the museum is afloat on the quayside nearby: in the 1918 sailboat *Santa Eulàlia*, which can be boarded.
Av Drassanes 1. Tel: 933 42 99 20. www.diba.es/mmaritim. Open: daily 10am–7pm. Admission charge. Metro: Drassanes. Bus: 14, 18, 59, 64.

Museu Nacional d'Art de Catalunya (MNAC)

The national museum of Catalan art, notable for its Romanesque collection (*see p101*).

Mirador Palau Nacional 6–10. Tel: 936 22 03 75. www.mnac.es. Open: Tue–Sat 10am–7pm, Sun 10am–2.30pm. Admission charge. Metro: Espanya. Bus: 50, 55.

Museu Picasso

The most-visited museum in Barcelona and one of the most attractive. Spread across five medieval palaces, it contains the largest collection in the world of the artist's formative years, as well as some from the Blue Period and (from his later work) the famous studies of Las Meninas.

Montcada 15–23. Tel: 933 19 6310. www.museupicasso.bcn.es. Open: Tue–Sat 10am–8pm, Sun 10am–3pm. Closed: Mon. Admission charge. Metro: Jaume I. Bus: 14, 17, 36, 64.

Museu Tèxtil i d'Indumentària

Housed in one of the many palaces in this medieval street, the textile museum has a small but attractive collection. The café in its courtyard and shop are both worth a pause.

Montcada 12–14. Tel: 933 19 76 03. www.museutextil.bcn.es. Open: Tue–Sat 10am–6pm, Sun 10am–3pm. Closed: Mon. Admission charge. Metro: Jaume I. Bus: 14, 17, 36, 64.

The MACBA, Museum of Contemporary Art, in the Raval district

Getting Away From It All

Golden beaches, sturdy castles, wine houses, wetlands, medieval towns and modern resorts are all easily accessible, and help visitors get a feel for the region from which Barcelona has grown. From Dalí's eccentricities in the north to Port Aventura in the south, there is something for everyone to enjoy.

A quiet square in Girona

CISTERCIAN ROUTE (LA RUTA DEL CISTER)

A 'triangle' of handsome Cistercian monasteries lies just inland from Tarragona among vineyards, almond and olive groves. Founded in the wake of the Counts of Barcelona as they took southern (or 'New') Catalonia from the Moors in the 12th century, they are havens of peace and tranquillity. Ideally reached by car, but check with the local tourist office for current tours.

Monestir de Poblet

Grandest of them all is the Monestir de Poblet, which also served as a royal palace and pantheon. Set in tranquil countryside 10km (6 miles) from Montblanc, its golden stones hide a complete community of buildings that make it the largest inhabited monastery in Europe. It is now a UNESCO World Heritage Site with 180,000 visitors a year. Like most Catalan religious houses, it has been severely set upon in its time: by the French in the War of Independence and by locals in the 19th-century Carlist Wars. In 1953 the sculptor Frederic Marès, who created the eclectic museum in Barcelona named after him, reconstructed the tombs, and today a couple of dozen monks are fortunate to have their home in this fully restored gem.
Tel: 977 87 12 47. Open daily. Admission charge.

Monestir de Santes Creus

The church in this monastery, nearest to Tarragona by the village of Valls, is a perfect example of Cistercian architecture, though it was not completed until the 18th century. It has the tomb of Jaume II (1291–1327) and its cloisters show the first sign of Gothic in Catalan. It is the only one of the three not to be used by a religious order, and its rooms are therefore more accessible.
Tel: 977 63 83 29. Open daily, except Mon. Tue free.

Vallbona de Les Monges

The smallest of the three and the only one in a village, which has the same name. It has been in continuous occupation by Cistercian nuns since 1157, and contains the tomb of Violant of Hungary, Jaume I's queen.
Tel: 973 33 02 66. Open daily, except Mon & Sun mornings.

COSTA BRAVA

The Costa Brava, the 'wild coast', is one of the most attractive in the Mediterranean, with pine-backed coves, soaring cliffs and sandy beaches. It begins at **Blanes**, where the terrain forces the railway from Barcelona inland, and continues north to the French border 67km (42 miles) away. Trains run to Blanes, Girona and Figueres, where there are bus connections to the rest of the coast. Hiring a car for a day or two is another option.

The major resorts are **Lloret de Mar**, **Tossa de Mar** and **Platja D'Aro**, all with good beaches and plenty of hotels. More intimate are the resorts and coves around **Palafrugell**, such as **Calella**, **Lafranc**, **Tamariu** and **Aiguablava** where there is a Parador and the Hotel Aiguablava, the most famous on the coast. Just inland are the historic medieval towns of **Pals** and **Peratalada**, good places to stop for lunch.

The biggest expanse of beach is the golden scimitar of the **Bay of Roses**. This is where the Greeks and Romans first set foot in Spain, at **Empúries**, and the remains of their 'emporium', with the Greek harbour wall, can be visited, as can the Iberian settlement of **Ullastret** near Pals.

At the top of the bay is the resort of **Roses** and the three-Michelin-star **El Bulli**, voted by *Restaurant Magazine* as the best restaurant in the world. *Cala Montjoi, Roses. Tel: 972 15 04 57. elbulli.com. Open: Apr–Sept.*

Roses is on the last folds of the Pyrenees. Just beyond, over a zig-zag mountain road, is Spain's most easterly

The Teatro–Museu Dalí in Figueres

town, **Cadaqués**, the St Tropez of Spain in the 1960s and still with a wealthy, hippy air. It has also become synonymous with Salvador Dalí. *www.costabrava.org.*

DALÍ COUNTRY

The three Dalí museums lie around the Empordà plain beneath the Pyrenees. The main market town of **Figueres** is a couple of hours from Barcelona by RENFE train (Plaça de Catalunya) and a TGV (starting 2004) takes 39 minutes. There are bus connections to the other Dalí haunts, though a hire car may be more convenient.

Teatro–Museu Dalí

Dalí (*see pp146–7*) was born in Figueres and in 2003 the council bought the house of his birth, Carrer Monturiol 6, with a view to making it a museum. But it is his own museum in a former theatre that attracts most visitors to the town. Not all the works on display are

The attractive buildings of Girona's old town rise above the River Onyar

his own, but most of the jokes are (do not miss the Mae West Room or the Rainy Cadillac) and so is the whole concept of the bread-roll plastered building. He is buried here and it is a fitting monument.
Tel: 972 67 75 00. www.salvador-dali.org. Open daily. Closed: Mon, Oct–June. Admission charge.

Casa–Museu Salvador Dalí

Dalí and his wife Gala spent most of their time in Portlligat on the coast just outside Cadaqués, and their former home is a delightful museum, the Casa–Museu Salvador Dalí, reached by a tourist train from Cadaqués. Evolved from two fishermen's cottages in this unspoilt bay, it is an enchanting place, proving he may have been a better interior designer than a painter. There

are many small touches, such as the bed positioned to make him the first person in Spain to see the sun rise each day.
Tel: 972 25 10 15. www.salvador-dali.org. Open daily. Closed: Mon, Oct–Mar. Tickets should be reserved 1–2 days in advance.

Casa–Museu Castell Gala Dalí

At Púbol 40km (25 miles) from Figueres, Dalí's 'gift to Gala' once again shows his great taste and flair for interiors, with some of his work on the walls of this three-storey 14th-century castle, which he restored. A collection of Gala's 'gala' dresses is also on permanent exhibition. She lived here on and off from 1971, when they bought it, and she is buried here. Dalí moved in after her death before his last years spent in the tower of his museum in Figueres.

Tel: 972 48 86 55. www.salvador-dali.org.
Open daily. Closed: Mon, Sept–Mar.
The castle is 4km (2.5 miles) from Flaça
station on the Figueres line. A bus stop
at Flaça is 2km (1 mile) from Púbol.

GIRONA

Girona is a Barcelona in the provinces
and a day can easily be passed exploring
its calm museums and shady medieval
streets. Trains leave regularly from Plaça
Catalunya in Barcelona and take about
an hour.

From the carp-filled River Onyar,
Girona's old town rises above earth-
coloured waterfront houses. A stone
bridge beside them leads to the
attractive **Rambla** and the start of
the old town. Through its heart is
Via Augusta, the Roman road that ran
from Rome, through France and down
to Tarragona (*see pp144–5*). Behind this
ancient lane is the Jewish Quarter or
Call, now the **Centre Bonastruc Ça
Porta**. This was home to several hundred
Jews from the late 9th century until their
expulsion in 1492.

Approached through the door in
an alley, Carrer de Sant Llorenç, which
was the only entrance to the quarter,
it is open every day and is a centre of
research and learning.

Via Augusta leaves the town under
an arch where the Angel of Good Death
looked down on those taken from the
city to be hanged. Just before the arch
a magnificent flight of steps rises to
the imposing **cathedral**, pure Catalan
Gothic, with the widest nave in
Christendom. Its museum contains
some beautiful artefacts, including
The Creation, a stunning 11th-century

A typical *cala*, cove, in the rugged Costa Brava

tapestry. In the neighbouring former
Episcopal Palace is the **Museu d'Art**,
with a rich collection of Romanesque
and Gothic church art.

The city museum, the **Museu
d'Història de la Ciutat**, is in a former
Capuchin convent, with a display of
instruments showing the evolution of
sardana music. Across the river in the
new town is the **Museu del Cinema**
(*Carrer Sequia 1*), with exhibits going
back to the 19th century.

To get a good view of the town take
the **Passeig Archaeològic** behind the
cathedral, which runs along the top
of the medieval walls.

MONTSERRAT

The holy high spot for Catalan
Christians is the mountain of
Montserrat and the monastery where
its famous choir sings twice a day. The
FFC train from Plaça Espanya to Aeri
de Montserrat takes an hour and from
there a cable car completes the journey.

Montserrat, the Holy Mountain, where Catalan Christians come to touch the black Madonna

Montserrat ('serrated mountain') is a truly rugged outcrop of dozens of rocky fingers poking up to 1,236m (4,055ft). Scattered over it are chapels and hermits' caves, but at its centre is a monastery and basilica where **La Moreneta**, the Black Virgin of Montserrat, patroness of Catalonia, is venerated.

Although the monastery dates from the 9th century, today's buildings are disappointingly modern, as the whole place was destroyed by the French in 1811 when Napoleon's forces hunted down the monks and hermits 'like goats'. Nevertheless, the sheer setting of the place, rebuilt and repopulated by Benedictine monks in 1844, remains dramatic.

La Moreneta stands behind the altar protected by glass, and pilgrims come to touch her orb. She is reputed to have been made by St Luke, brought here by St Peter in AD 50, and later hidden in a cave (the **Santa Cova**, which can be visited via a funicular railway, as can the hermitage of St John). Modern science says that she dates from the 12th century.

There are shops, cafés and a hotel in the complex. A museum has a hotch-potch of paintings, relics and liturgical items. Try to get here in time to hear the monastery hymn, *Virolai*, at 1pm. *Salve Regina* is sung at 7.10pm. The choir takes a break in July and over the Christmas period. A CD is a suitable souvenir. *Tel: 938 35 02 51. Open daily.*

PORT AVENTURA

Just south of Tarragona near the resort of **Salou** is Port Aventura one of the biggest adventure theme parks in Europe, which will keep children amused and spending money all day. Run by Universal Studios, it stretches across more than 1sq km of elaborate scenery re-creating five areas from around the world. These are the Great Wall of China, with what is claimed to be the biggest roller coaster ride in continental Europe, a Polynesian paradise, ruins of Mayan Mexico, a Mediterranean idyll and the Wild West where cowboys enact an *estampida*. *Tel: 977 77 90 00. www.portaventura.es. Open daily. Closed: mid-Jan–mid-Mar. Port Aventura has its own railway station, reached form Barcelona via Tarragona. One hour by car.*

SITGES

For a taste of the seaside beyond Barcelona, head for Sitges, 35km (22 miles) south of the city and easily

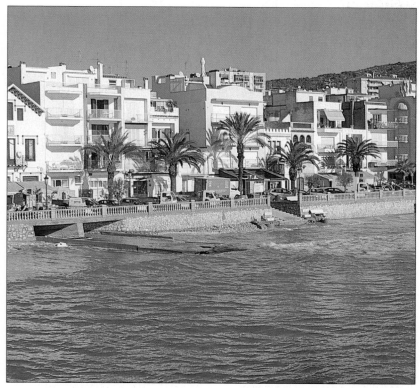

One of the beaches at Sitges, a popular place for Barcelonans to go for Sunday lunch

Museu Cau Ferrat, former home of the artist Santiago Rusiñol

the **Museu Cau Ferrat**. Sited above the sea, it has an intriguing collection of paintings, ceramics and ironwork. Opposite is the **Museu Maricel**, another lovely building, with murals by Josep Maria Sert. There is also a **Museu Romàntic** in the town, which has been restored with a 19th-century domestic interior.

TARRAGONA

When the Romans conquered the Iberian peninsula they divided it into three provinces. The Eastern one was Tarraconensis (Tarragona), and it is the best place in Catalonia to see Roman remains. Trains run directly from Barcelona and take about two hours.

The Museu Maricel (sea and sky) has murals by Josep Maria Sert

reached by train from Plaça Catalunya. It has been popular with Barcelonans for nearly two centuries, and it remains elegant, exuberant and relaxed, with clean, golden beaches, excellent restaurants and numerous lively bars. It also has a flourishing gay population which dominates the outrageous annual pre-Lent carnival.

The pretty fishing village was taken up by 19th-century artists, whose use of blues and pinks gave them the name of 'Luminists', and it was Santiago Rusiñol (1861–1931), a founder of the *modernista* Quatre Gats café in Barcelona, who put the town on the art map when he bought an El Greco painting and paraded it through the streets to his house, now

The Rambla in Tarragona comes to a dead halt above the sea, which gives it the name of 'the balcony of Europe'. From here you can look down on the Roman **amphitheatre**, still largely intact. Behind it is the **Museu Nacional Arqueològic**, which has a large collection of Roman artefacts. But to feel the might of the Roman empire, walk along the kilometre that remains of the Roman wall, built of stones of such size it is hard to know how it was possible to cut and place them here. The Gothic **cathedral** with a tranquil cloister of orange trees is also worth visiting. A steep hill leads down to the Serallo part of the old port, and here there are excellent fish restaurants where a meal can be washed down with Tarragona's fine wine.

VIC

The best time to visit this inland town is market day, Tuesday or Saturday, when stalls fill the unusually large, arcaded main square and rural characters crowd the streets. Here you can buy the town's speciality, a salami called *fuet*.

The **cathedral**, remodelled in a neoclassical style in the 19th century, has a grand Romanesque tower, and murals painted by Josep Maria Sert (who decorated the Rockefeller Center in New York). Enormous figures from the Bible form theatrical tableaux on the walls, which he painted twice: the first attempt did not survive the Civil War. Sert is buried in the 14th-century cloister. The adjoining **Museu Episcopal** has the finest collection of Romanesque art outside Barcelona. The town has an atmospheric medieval Plaça Major.

WINE ROUTE

The wines of Catalonia are some of the most interesting in Spain (*see p167*). A speciality is *cava*, a Champagne-method wine, and the heart of its production is **Sant Sadurní d'Anoia**, 45 minutes by train from Plaça de Catalunya. The house of Freixenet produces some 80 per cent of Catalunya's *cava* and there are tours regularly throughout the day. *Tel: 938 91 70 00.*

Codorníu, the house that 'invented' *cava*, has a beautiful *modernista* factory, with a museum of posters and related graphic art, as well as tours.
Tel: 938 18 32 32.

Nearby **Vilafranca del Penedès** is the centre for still wine and a **Museu del Vi** is housed in the 14th-century royal palace. The tourist office gives details of all the bodegas and producers that can be visited in the area.
Tel: 938 90 05 82. Open: 10am–2pm & 4–7pm, Sun 10am–2pm. Closed: Mon. Admission charge.

WETLAND WILDLIFE

The **Parc Natural del Delta d'Ebre** covers 70sq km (27sq miles) at the mouth of Spain's longest river, the Ebre. This nature reserve is one of the most important wildlife habitats in Europe. It is best to visit by car, perhaps combining it with a visit to Tarragona or Port Aventura. Get your bearings in the Eco-Museu in Deltebre, and follow the recommended routes.

The marshlands at **Empúria-brava** on the Costa Brava are also an important wildlife site, and you might see flamingos, black-winged stilts, egrets and herons.

Salvador Dalí

Salvador Dalí i Domènech was born in 1904 in Figueres, the market town of the Alt Empordà, where his father was a notary. For their holidays the family visited the coast at Cadaqués 25km (17 miles) away, and the two places remained with him all his life. In particular the rocky coast around Cap Creu can be seen in many of his paintings.

In 1921 he went to the Escuella de Belles Artes in Madrid where he befriended two other students, Spain's great 20th-century poet Federico Garcia Lorca and Luis Bunuel, with whom he would make the two most famous Surrealist films, *Le Chien Andalu* (1928) and *L'Age d'Or* (1930).

With encouragement from both Picasso and Miró, Dalí went to Paris to seek his fame and fortune and it was here that, in 1929, he met André Breton and joined the Surrealists. Five years later he was famously ejected from the group, wearing a diver's helmet and several jerseys for the occasion. Surrealism looked to the subconscious and the works of Sigmund Freud, though after the father of psychiatry met Dalí he pronounced him 'a typical Spaniard – totally mad'. Dalí invented for himself the 'paranoiac-critical method' of looking at the world.

The same year that he joined the Surrealists he met Gala, the Russian wife of the French poet Paul Eluard, and they remained together for the rest of their lives. In 1930 he found and bought the fisherman's cottage at Portlligat, his home for the next 50 years. At the start of the Civil War he left for America, making his name (and the name Breton conjured for him from an anagram – *avida dollars*) with paintings, sculptures, lithographs and designs. He returned to Portlligat in 1948, having stated, to the fury of his artistic peers, that Franco had 'saved Spain'.

During the 1960s his hallucinatory images struck a chord with dreamy hippies and Cadaqués soon became the trendiest place in Spain. Rumours of the goings-on in Dalí's Portlligat house were rampant. In 1974, with the assistance of the local authorities, he turned the run-down local theatre in Figueres into a museum, and when it opened it met with instant success.

His work tailed off in later years, and there were rumours that, as a final Surrealist joke, he had signed many blank canvases. His whole life was as much about art as his paintings, his public appearances always something of an event. In the end, after the death of Gala (whose body he failed to eat, as promised), he shut himself away in the tower of his museum in Figueres, which became his mausoleum on his death in 1989.

The Fundació Gala–Salvador, which was set up six years before his death, has been active in promoting his works in Spain and around the world. In its trust are more than 4,000 artworks and one of its patrons is Princess Cristina of Spain.

Opposite and above: Views of the Dalí Museum in Figueres, where the artist is buried

Shopping

Leading design store Vinçon once bore the logo 'I shop therefore I am' on its perennially stylish carrier bags. To see the crowds massing in the main shopping streets around Plaça Catalunya on Saturdays and tourists returning home laden with extra bags suggests it is a universal philosophy. At least in Barcelona shopping sprees can be relieved by a drink on a terrace or an occasional tapa.

Everything is available in El Corte Inglés

What to buy

The unrelenting march of globalisation has inevitably reduced the differences, so international chains are beginning to proliferate here and Catalan or Spanish labels are more available elsewhere in the world. However there is more choice here of national brands, and at more affordable prices, and for the moment the smaller businesses are just holding their own. So you can find the 'corner shops' in most districts still selling their own specialities, be it food, hardware, fans, wickerwork or even lightning conductors. The Old Town, Gràcia and parts of the Eixample are best for these finds.

Ceramics

A speciality of the region, cheap, colourful and very practical in a kitchen. Heavy to carry home but well worth it. The brown cooking pots, *cassoles*, can be found in supermarkets and hardware stores as well as the ceramic shops.

La Caixa de Fang

Wide attractive range of pots including some from other parts of Spain. Their olive-wood cooking utensils are a lighter gift alternative.
Freneria 1.

Molsa

Pots, plates and trinkets as well as valuable antique ceramics.
Plaça Sant Josep Oriol.

Design

A recurrent theme in Barcelona (*see pp70–71*). A Gaudí chair may not fit in your luggage but an oil decanter would, or a Santa & Cole lamp.

Bd Ediciones de Diseño

Best of 20th-century and contemporary design in an exquisite space.
Mallorca 291.

Pilma

Stylish home design including suitcases and jewellery
Av Diagonal 403.

Vinçon

No self-respecting designer home in Barcelona would be without something from here.
Passeig de Gràcia 96.

Fashion

Internationally known local designers tend to have shops in the Eixample.

Adolfo Dominguez

The Galician who made crushed linen fashionable is one of Spain's best-known designers. For men and women.
Passeig de Gràcia 32.

Antonio Miró

Still a leader in Catalan fashion. Toni Miró's clothes for men and women are understated and stylish.
Consell de Cent 349.

Cannibal

In an ancient candle shop. Valenciana Angeles Salvador's easy-to-wear original clothes in wonderful materials, for men and women.
Carme 5.

David Valls

Cool, comfortable styles from this Catalan whose medium is knitwear.
València 235.

Instinto

Individual designs for women in appealing colours and comfortable styles, at an accessible price.
Banys Nous 5.

Jean Pierre Bua

Intimate shop with good atmosphere, yet it has the widest range of international labels you will find in Barcelona.
Diagonal 469.

The lesser-known designers have small boutiques, especially in the Old Town.

High-street fashion at accessible prices is everywhere. Best streets are Pelai, Portaferrisa, Portal del Angel, or the large shopping centres. **Zara** (*at least nine branches in Barcelona*) is the Spanish fashion phenomenon of the century, with high turnover and effective, cheap fashion for men, women and children. An offshoot of the empire targeted at teenagers is **Bershka** (*Portal del Angel 15*). **Oysho** (*Pelai 46*) has tangas, tops and things to lounge in. Other chains with branches all over town are **Mango**, which is a cut above Zara, and **System Action**.

Window shopping can be mouth watering

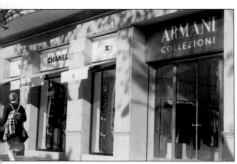

Passeig de Gràcia and Diagonal are for elegant shopping

Food
The best and freshest is in the markets. (*For other specialities see pp172–3.*)

Jewellery
Freya
Tiny shop in Gràcia bursting with colourful jewellery cheap enough to treat yourself.
Verdi 17.

Hipòtesi
Stylish quality pieces from local designers and frequent exhibitions of foreign talent in this attractive shop, with manageable prices.
Rambla Catalunya 105.

Leather
Leather is still a good deal. Discount clothes shops can be found on La Rambla, while Loewe remains exclusive. Shoes and handbags range from the cheap and cheerful to top designs like Muxart. The pedestrian street Portal del Angel and Portaferrisa which it leads into have a high concentration of shoe shops.

Sought-after Camper, the shoe makers from Mallorca, have their own outlets but are also found in other shoe shops.

Camper
Original shoe design, chunky, comfortable and very well made.
Valencia 249.

Loewe
Elegant expensive leather from gloves to full-length coats.
Passeig de Gràcia 35.

Muxart
Shoes, boots and bags that are like works of art.
Rambla de Catalunya 47.

Tascón
Good range of the best shoe manufacturers in small appealing shop.
Passeig de Gràcia 53.

Markets
Weekly, seasonal and annual markets are traditional, selling everything from goat's cheese to antique books (*see pp152–3*).

Souvenirs and miscellaneous
For Barça football shirts, Spanish dolls or magnetic paella dishes, La Rambla is the place. For more alternative gift ideas or mementoes try the following.

La Botiga de la Virreina
Barcelona-inspired classy souvenirs from Gaudí 'pavement tile' soap to Miró mouse mats.
La Rambla 99.

Casa Oliveres
One of the few traditional lace shops remaining.
Daguería 11.

Cereria Subirá
Candles in all shapes and sizes in this candle shop with a history going back to 1762.
Baixada Llibreteria 7.

Gràfiques El Tinell
In the shadows of the cathedral, an old print shop selling cards, engravings and ex-libris stickers.
Frenería 1.

MACBA (contemporary art museum) shop
Inspiring ideas from designer pan scourers to Barba Corsini chairs.
Plaça dels Angels 1.

La Pedrera shop
Classy souvenirs with a predominantly Gaudí theme.
Provença 261–265.

Sports
Decathlon
Sports equipment at affordable prices including rental of bikes, roller blades and skis.
Plaça Vila de Madrid 1; also in L'Illa.

Traditional fashion
Shops to visit for their charm.

Alonso
Small *modernista* shop crammed with fans, gloves and shawls.
Santa Anna 27.

La Manual Alpargatera
Traditional rope-soled sandals in wide range of styles and colours made on the spot.
Avinyó 7.

Obach
Classic hat shop from 1920s now run by third generation.
Call 2.

Department stores
El Corte Inglés
Still going strong, Spain's main department store where everything can be found. The supermarket is high quality and well stocked with imported goods. The branch in Portal del Angel specializes in sports, books and music.
Plaça Catalunya 14; Av Diagonal 617.

Shopping malls
Ever on the increase, exhausting but air-conditioned and practical if you are short of time.

Diagonal Mar
The newest shopping centre, and the nearest to the beach.
Diagonal 3–35.

L'Illa
The most sophisticated of them all, designed by Rafael Moneo.
Diagonal 545–557.

El Triangle
One whole corner of the square was taken over to build this. Worth visiting for FNAC, a multi-level book, music and computer store. Open until 10pm.
Plaça Catalunya.

Markets

Despite increasingly frenzied lifestyles and the growth of the hypermarket culture, Barcelona's fidelity to Mediterranean street life and to good eating is reflected in its wonderful and numerous food markets. Each of the city's neighbourhoods has its own municipal indoor food market, and *cuina de mercat* – cuisine using fresh seasonal produce from the market – is a genre of its own developed into a first-rate culinary art by creative chefs.

The market to end all markets, of course, is the famed Boquería (also known as Mercat de Sant Josep), the inner sanctum of Barcelona's food universe, where the top chefs buy their produce early in the morning. Soaring 19th-century iron architecture provides a cathedral-like setting for this cornucopia of colour and bustle, a feast of sounds and sights and smells.

Several neighbourhood markets are worth a visit, and morning is the best time. The Mercat de La Concepció in the Eixample is a splendid example of late 19th-century architecture in the *modernista* style. By contrast, the Mercat de la Llibertat in Gràcia is small, squashed, intimate and utterly authentic. The food markets also contain bars and bakeries, cooked food and organic produce, and most are surrounded by street stalls, always good for a browse and a bargain. Sant Antoni (the only market in the Eixample built according to Cerdà's original plan) vies with the Boqueria and Catalina for the distinction of being the oldest.

Seasonal markets are also an institution, in particular the picturesque Fira de Santa Llúcia, held during the run-up to Christmas in the Plaça de la Catedral where locals flock to buy hand-made crib-figures, Christmas trees and other traditional trappings.

Barcelona also has a number of traditional outdoor markets such as the popular second-hand book fair on Sunday mornings at the Mercat de Sant Antoni, which also offers magazines, video games, pins and related paraphernalia. Sunday morning is also a must for stamp and coin enthusiasts at the market in the Barri Gòtic's imposing Plaça Reial, while one weekend each month there is an art fair in the Plaça Sant Josep Oriol.

The wondrous assortment of junk and jumble at Barcelona's well-loved flea market, Els Encants, is another institution, and makes a change from the dizzy heights of leading-edge design. If you are really after bargains, make sure you get there early in the morning (many stalls pack up at lunchtime) and watch out for pickpockets. On Thursdays the antiques and bric-a-brac people set up shop under white canopies opposite the cathedral. Relatively new is the weekend antiques and bric-a-brac fair on the waterfront, at the bottom of the Rambla. Have a good rummage – or retire to refuel and watch the human comedy at one of the many strategic café terraces.

Opposite and above: Whether you shop at La Boqueria (left) or your local market, the produce is at its freshest and best

Entertainment

If you really do need more than the free entertainment on the streets, the changing spectacle of La Rambla or the musicians playing Bach or Blues around the cathedral in the Gothic quarter, to say nothing of the spontaneous Capoeira sessions down by the seafront, or the Andean music on Plaça Catalunya, then read on. There is plenty on offer, from fringe to mainstream, from guitar festivals to festivals of ancient music.

Festival of the Sea

Check local listings, including the weekly magazine *Guia del Ocio*, the daily press and the official Barcelona city agenda at *www.bcn.es*. The English-language magazine *Metropolitan* is available free in various hotels, bookshops, the Palau de la Virreina, bars and cafés.

Nightlife

Trendy bars go in and out of fashion before you can say Jordi Labanda. The

The many cinemas offer a wide choice of films, some in original language

only solution to getting to the hippest spots is to follow the crowd. Try the up-and-coming areas around Joaquim Costa and Ferlandina, just beyond the MACBA (contemporary art museum); also the Old Town in and around Plaça Reial, Plaça George Orwell and Avinyó (*see also pp76–7*). Some favourites are listed here:

Almirall

Laid-back generation in a *modernista* setting dating from 1860.
Joaquín Costa 33.

Benidorm

As kitzch as the name suggests, but cool.
Joaquín Costa 35.

Café Royale

Sophisticated lounge-bar with good music; relaxing.
Nou de Zurbano 3.

Glaciar

A bustling cathedral of a bar with great atmosphere.
Pl Reial 3.

Live music/dance

There are speciality venues but many places have a fusion of styles – a live concert until 1am then DJ sounds, for example. A jazz club will sometimes play flamenco. Check local listings for programmes. Here are some well-established night spots:

Bikini

Just celebrated its 50th anniversary though now in new venue. Good selection of music.
Deu i Mata 105.

Cibeles

Córcega 363. Tel: 93 317 79 94.

Harlem Jazz Club

Nothing pretentious about this intimate jazz club that runs the Festival de Jazz of the Old Town every year.
Comtessa de Sobradiel 8.
Tel: 93 310 07 55.

Jamboree

Long established jazz club revived in the 1990s has good contemporary programming.
Plaça Reial 17. Tel: 93 301 75 64.

London Bar

Jazz, blues, Brazilian, plus cabaret and circus acts.
Nou de la Rambla 34. Tel: 93 318 52 61.

Luz de Gas

Old music hall. Pretty location for jazz and blues concerts.
Muntaner 246.

La Paloma

If you go nowhere else, be sure to spend an evening in this 'Palace of Dance'.
Tigre 27. Tel: 93 301 68 97.

Razzmatazz, Sala 1

Almogàvers 122. Tel: 93 320 82 00.
www.salarazzmatazz.com.

Razzmatazz, Sala 2 y 3

Apart from concerts, becomes the Loft Club at 1am at weekends.
Pamplona 88. www.theloftclub.com.

Sala Apolo

Nou de la Rambla 113.

Los Tarantos

Flamenco is not indigenous to Catalonia so beware of tourist traps – but Los Tarantos has one of the most authentic flamenco shows. Show begins at 10pm. Book in advance if possible.
Plaça Reial 17. Tel: 93 318 30 67.

Pubs

Nearly every district has its Irish pub now, but the majority are in the Old Town, as well as some other pubs. Very popular when important football matches are being played. Here are just a few:

The Clansman

This one is Scottish. Check the malts.
Vigatans 13.

Fastnet

A cross between a Barceloneta café overlooking the port and a pub serving English food.
Passeig Joan de Borbó.

John Martin

Wide selection of draught Belgian beer.
Ases 16.

P. Flaherty

Brunches and a large screen for
unmissable finals.
Plaça Joaquim Xirau.

The Quiet Man

Live music, Guinness, Irish of course.
Marquès de Barberà 11.

Cinema

Most popular commercial films
are dubbed into Spanish or Catalan,
but there are several cinemas which
specialise in *v.o.* (*versión original*) and
show films in the original language.
These cinemas, listed below, tend to
have the most interesting film selection.
Also check the listings in newspapers
or magazines, where it will identify
whether a film is being shown in its
original version.

Maldà

A favourite: two-film programme that
changes weekly. Good for catching up
on films you missed the first time
round.
Carrer del Pí 5. Tel: 93 317 85 29.

Renoir Floridablanca

Floridablanca 135. Tel: 902 22 16 22.
www.entradas.com.

Billboards everywhere announce forthcoming events

Verdi and **Verdi Park**
Both have good programming and
multi-screens.
Verdi: Verdi 32. Tel: 93 238 79 90.
Verdi Park: Torrijos 49. Tel: 93 238 79 90.

Yelmo Cineplex Icària
In the Centre de la Vila shopping centre
in Vila Olímpica. 15 screens. Sessions
begin at 11am and at weekends there
are 1am sessions.
Salvador Espriu 61. Tel: 902 22 09 22.

Theatre
With the resurgence of the Catalan
language, most plays are in Catalan.
Occasionally theatre companies from
other parts of Spain visit. There are
some small English-language theatre
companies who perform on the
alternative circuit. If leading Catalan
company Els Joglars are playing do not
miss them: brilliant, scathing theatre that
can be understood despite the language.
Also worth catching Els Comediants
(very colourful visual theatre) and the
hilarious Cubana company from Sitges.

Mercat de les Flors
A mixed programme often including
more visual theatre, new techniques,
mime etc so worth checking out. Often
the venue for foreign companies.
Lleida 59. Tel: 93 426 18 75.
www.mercatflors.com.

Teatre Nacional de Catalunya
Excellent standard of theatre,
monumental venue, mostly Catalan.
Their dance programme is worth
watching out for, in summer months.
Plaça de les Arts 1. Tel: 93 3306 57 00.

Tivoli
Charming old theatre. Often has
flamenco shows, visiting stars and more
accessible productions. Well worth
checking out..
Casp 8. Tel: 93 412 20 63.

Opera
Gran Teatre del Liceu
Tickets for next season (which begins in
September) go on sale in July, but there
are usually some available throughout
the year, or cancellations on the day of
performance. Purchase through
Servicaixa (*see box on p159*) or
www.liceubarcelona.com, or at the ticket
office located in the theatre. *See also
pp82–3.*
La Rambla 51–59. Tel: 93 485 99 13.

The Tivoli is one of the city's oldest and prettiest
theatres

Classical music

The concert halls have a busy repertoire complemented by different festivals which often take place in the same venues: Festival de Guitarra, Festival de Jazz, Festival de Música Antiga (ancient music). Concerts are occasionally held in the CCCB (*Montalegre 5*), the Caixa Forum on Montjuïc and also in the churches Santa Maria del Mar, Santa Maria del Pí and Sant Felip Neri, all in the Gothic quarter.

L'Auditori

Sophisticated new concert hall near the National Theatre.
Lepant 150. Tel: 93 247 93 00.

Palau de la Música Catalana

Worth going whatever the concert for the experience of this wild *modernista* music hall designed by Domènech i Montaner.
Sant Francesc de Paula 2.
Tel: 93 268 10 00.

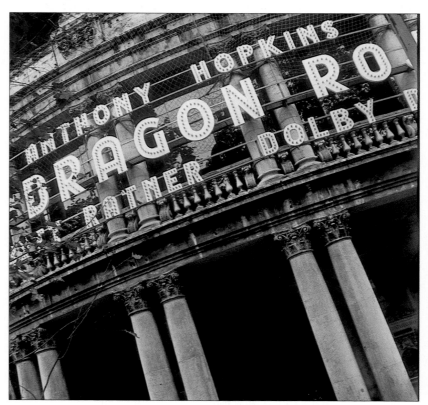

Major international films are usually dubbed into Spanish or Catalan (*see p156*)

Ballet and dance

The Liceu opera house has a short ballet season, and some visiting companies perform in other theatres. Modern dance can be seen in the Mercat de les Flors, Teatre Nacional (*see p157*) or at L'Espai (*Travessera de Gràcia 63. Tel: 93 414 31 33*).

Rock concerts

Barcelona is a favourite stopping place for most European tours, from heavy-metal bands to ageing legends from the 1960s. Mega concerts take place in the Palau Sant Jordi on Montjuïc, or in one of the outdoor stadiums. Tickets available through promoters (check listings), record shops in Tallers (just off La Rambla) and FNAC in El Triangle center in Plaça Catalunya. Book online (depending on the promoter) at *www.bbvaticket.com* or *www.ticktackticket.com*.

World music

Increasing number of tours of world music artistes. Favourite venues are La Paloma, Sala Apolo, Bikini, Palau de la Música (*see pp155 and 156 for addresses*).

Casino

Gran Casino de Barcelona. *Marina 19–21. Tel: 93 225 78 78.*

Bullfighting

Plaza de Toros Monumental
Not for the faint-hearted, nor the politically correct and what is more not even true to Catalan culture, but for anyone who wants to investigate this side of Spanish culture the only bullring still open in Barcelona is worth a visit. The Monumental was built early in the 20th century as its decorative, tiled façade suggests. Bullfighting season is from April to October. Out of season it is often used by visiting circuses. (*Gran Via 747. Tel 93 245 58 02*).

TICKET SALES

Many theatres, cinemas, concert halls and other shows centralise their ticket sales through two main telephone agencies:

Tel-Entrada
Tel: 902 10 12 12. www.telentrada.com.
(Caixa de Catalunya savings bank)

Servicaixa
Tel: 902 33 22 11 or with credit card in Servicaixa machines found in some branches of La Caixa savings bank.

A designer bar complete with snooker table

Children

Travelling with children in Barcelona is relatively easy as Catalans adore them, and small children are still *los reyes de la casa* – in other words the 'kings' or centre of the household. They are welcomed in restaurants, indulged in shops and markets, and often found playing in plazas until late at night, particularly on hot summer evenings or during the different fiestas of Barcelona.

Several companies offer organised bike tours

The free entertainment for kids is boundless. If your visit coincides with one of the many fiestas you have hit the jackpot – huge papier-mâché figures, *gegants*, come out and parade the streets along with mythical beasts and fire-spitting dragons. Processions with

La Rambla street artist

municipal brass bands on horseback, people on stilts and colourful floats tour around the city. Extra fairgrounds mushroom all over the place.

Even without fiestas children love all the spectacles on La Rambla – magicians, statues, clowns, puppets. Activities are often organised for them in the Rambla del Raval, the Plaça de la Catedral or public parks. Check the *infantil* section in local listings for any special events.

The beaches Barceloneta and Nova Icària have climbing frames like spider's webs and behind Platja Nova Mar Bella is a *half*, as they call it here, for skateboarders and roller-bladers. Windsurfboards can be rented on the beach.

The best park for children is the Ciutadella (*see pp102–7*) with a duck pond, rowing boats, a small games park for the tiny, spontaneous drumming sessions at weekends, and of course the zoo – always a hit. Nearby in Passeig de Picasso 40 you can rent a family bike made for four, or individual ones. The Collserola woods (*see pp122–3*) are great for rambles and picnics.

Aquàrium

Situated on Port Vell, in the Maremagnum complex, this huge aquarium delights kids, especially the sharks. There are also specimens from cold and tropical river waters, penguins, piranhas and alligators. The aquarium has more than 50 interactive items.
Tel: 93 221 74 74.
www.aquariumbcn.com. Open: daily 9am–9pm.

Cable car

A great trip for everyone, though adults usually get more anxious than kids. Unimaginable peace as you glide over the harbour to the Torre Sant Sebastià, which now has a swish restaurant at a great height. Be sure to choose a clear day for the spectacular views.
Torre de Jaume I, Moll de Barcelona.

Family concerts

The Caixa Forum, L'Auditori and El Liceu opera house all have excellent music programmes for children on Saturday and Sunday mornings. See local listings. The CCCB, Fundació Joan Miró and Teatre Poliorama also have cultural programmes tailored for children at weekends.

Golondrinas

These charming wooden pleasure boats originated in the 1888 Exposition and are still going strong. A quick trip to the sea wall and back, glimpsing the luxury cruise ships and the giant container vessels in the industrial port. More fun

The zoo in the Ciutadella is always a success with kids

than the newer catamaran which goes out to sea and to the Olympic Port.
Moll de Drassanes, near Columbus monument. Tel: 93 442 31 06.

Science museum (Museu de la Ciència Fundació la Caixa)

Wonderful, entertaining museum for all the family. Check whether it has reopened after extensive building work.
See pp135–6.

Zoo de Barcelona

Get there early to see the dolphin show (twice a day) and do not miss *Floquet de Neu* (Snowflake), the world's only albino gorilla in captivity, whose children are now being brought up in the zoo.
Parc de la Ciutadella.
Tel: 93 225 67 80.
www.zoobarcelona.com.
Open: daily 10am–7.30pm. Closes earlier in winter according to daylight.

Sport and Leisure

Not surprisingly, another area where the Olympic Games made its mark in the lives of Barcelonans was in sport. A dramatic increase in the number and standard of facilities has opened up a range of possibilities to a wider audience.

Dive into local activities in Barcelona!

Football is a consuming passion for most of the population, male and female. Otherwise, Catalans are not traditionally committed to practising sports, though they love to get out at weekends: skiing in winter, spending time on the beach and in the mountains in summer. Walking is an old tradition that forms part of the Catalan spirit: the *Centre Excursionista de Catalunya* in the Gothic quarter dates back to 1876, and it is common today to see groups of young people going off with backpacks on an excursion.

Organised sports have not been a priority – but now that seems to be changing as Catalans, along with the rest of Europe, seek a healthier lifestyle. The new passion is cycling, which is practised enthusiastically both in and out of the city. Specific cross-country cycling routes have been drawn up all over Catalonia.

Bowling
Pedralbes Bowling
All-American bowling alley in a modern part of town. Good for a rainy day.

A cool spot on a hot summer's day

Avinguda Doctor Marañón 11. Tel: 93 333 03 52. Open: daily 10am–2am.

Cycling
Filicletos
Child bikes, adult bikes, tandems, family bikes, child seats, all for rental.
Passeig de Picasso 40. Tel: 93 319 78 11.

Un Cotxe Menys ('one less car')
Good quality bikes for rent, and organised tours.
Esparteria 3. Tel: 93 268 21 05.

Mike's Bike Tours
Good tours on sturdy American bikes.
Plaça George Orwell. Tel: 93 301 36 12.

Bicycle rental is also available in various places and at weekends on Montjuïc as part of the M Card (*see p93*).

Golf
Golf courses are spreading fast across Catalonia. Within comparatively easy reach of Barcelona are the following two courses.

Golf courses are mushrooming all over Catalonia

El Prat

A premier course near the airport. Clubs can be hired.

El Prat de Llobregat. Tel: 93 379 02 78.

Club de Golf de Sant Cugat

Pleasant spot just behind Barcelona, only five minutes walk from the FGC station (20 minutes from Plaça Catalunya).

Sant Cugat del Vallès. Tel: 93 674 39 08.

Horse riding
Hipica Sant Cugat

Just outside Sant Cugat. Courses for beginners or day treks in the Collserola hills. Call in advance.

Finca la Palleria, Av Corts Catalanes, Sant Cugat. Tel: 93 674 83 85. Bus: A4 from FGC station.

Ice skating
Skating Pista de Gel

Large rink fairly central in Eixample.

Roger de Flor 168. Tel: 93 245 28 00. www.skatingbcn.com.

Swimming
Piscinas Bernat Picornell

Treat yourself to a swim in an Olympic pool. During Grec Summer festival they hold a swim + film season at night.

Av de l'Estadi 30–49. Tel: 93 423 40 41. www.picornell.com.

Banys Sant Sebastià

Huge indoor and attractive outdoor pools right on the beach. One of Barceloneta's first swimming pools totally rebuilt in the 1990's.

Plaça del Mar 1. Tel: 93 221 05 06.

Tennis
Centre Municipal Tennis Vall d'Hebron

The Vall d'Hebron, in the foothills of the Collserola range but easy to reach, was another important Olympic centre in 1992. Twenty-four courts

Petanca is one of the oldest, most entertaining spectator sports…

available to the public, but cannot be reserved.
Passeig Vall d'Hebron 178–196.
Tel: 93 427 65 00. www.fctennis.org.
Metro: line 3 Montbau.

Water sports
Centre Municipal de Vela
Sailing courses for children and adults. Rental of dinghies and windsurfers. Yacht charters for one day or longer.
Port Olímpic. Tel: 93 225 79 40.

Spectator sports
American Football
Barcelona's local team, the Barcelona Dragons, has a great following. Games are played in the Olympic stadium in Montjuïc.

Basketball
Second only to Barça the famed football team, Barça the basketball team are very popular especially since winning the European Cup in 2003. Part of Fútbol Club Barcelona, they play in the Palau Blaugrana.
Aristides Maillol 12–18. Tel: 93 496 36 00.
www.fcbarcelona.com.

Football
If you get a chance to see a match in Camp Nou, take it (*see pp132–3*). Difficult to get tickets for a match with arch rivals Real Madrid, but lesser matches should be possible.
Aristides Maillol 12–18. Tel: 93 496 36 00.
www.fcbarcelona.com.

Motor Sports
Major racing-car and motorbike events take place in the Circuit Catalunya in

Montmeló, near Granollers.
Tel: 93 571 97 00. www.circuitcat.com.

Petanca
Generally known as *boules* in other parts of Europe, this is the game played by old men in berets. Watching these characters and their technique is a peaceful way to spend an evening. Catch them in most public parks, or along Passeig Lluis Companys, near Arc de Triomf.

Tennis
The Reial Club de Tenis is an exclusive club where the annual Conde de Godó tournament is played.
Bosch i Gimpera 5. Tel: 93 203 78 52.

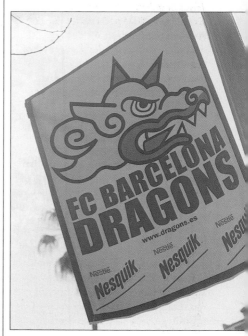

...and one of the newest, American football

Food and Drink

With a staggering 3,000 restaurants as well as innumerable bars and cafés which almost without exception serve something to eat, Barcelona offers wonderful food in surroundings for all seasons: convivial old taverns, sunny terraces, museum courtyards, the seafront and even the tip of the pier.

Trendy or traditional, the choice is infinite

A great many of the most emblematic restaurants are clustered in the Gothic Quarter and the Raval, with Barceloneta and the Olympic Port being a must for seafood and the sheer pleasure of eating outdoors, with a soothing view over the Port Vell to Montjuïc or out to sea. Many seafood restaurants offer a selection of tapas called *pica-pica* including crispy-fried vegetable titbits, sardines and croquettes to be dipped into piquant Romesco sauce.

Gràcia, too, is full of eating places, many of them very inexpensive as they are more off the beaten tourist track. While there are restaurants from other regions of Spain such as Galicia and the Basque country, the best bet is to go for Catalan–Mediterranean cuisine, or *cuina de mercat* or *cocina de mercado* (*see pp152–3*), which uses whatever is in season at the local market. Increasingly cosmopolitan, alongside more traditional French and Italian establishments, Barcelona has a growing number of restaurants from across the world, including Greek, Lebanese, Mexican, Thai, Chinese, Japanese, Brazilian. The choice for vegetarians is constantly

improving too. Catalonia also has its own version of fast food in the form of the *entrepà* or *bocata* (sandwich), a long fresh crusty loaf stuffed with ham, omelette, salad, tuna, etc. This is the fare offered by local chains such as Pans & Company.

Mealtimes

Lunch, the main meal of the day, is served at the earliest from about 1.30pm, with peak time from 2 till 4pm. Most restaurants in all price ranges offer a surprisingly economical *menú del dia* or set lunch, with even the most basic (just over €6) offering a choice of starter, main course of meat or fish, and dessert, plus drink.

For *berenar* or *merienda*, an afternoon snack taken at around 4 or 5pm, try a *granja* (milk bar) or one of the famous *pastisseries* (pastry shops). The *forn* (bakery) is also an institution. More and more of these places have reinvented themselves as stylish little cafeterias, and they are delightul for breakfast, elevenses and afternoon snacks, or for scrumptious pastries and sandwiches to take away to see you through to a late dinner from 9pm. Restaurants usually do not offer set menus for dinner, so be prepared to pay more – or 'do tapas' (*see pp174–5*). It is advisable to book in advance at some of the more upmarket restaurants, particularly for Fridays and weekends.

Wine

The Catalan wine industry is one of the most important in Spain, with a number of official D O regions (*Denominación de Origen*, the Spanish equivalent of the *Appellation Controlée*) such as Alella, known for its white wines, Penedès, the home of *cava*, and Priorat. Eating in Barcelona is a good opportunity to try out lesser known wines from the *carta de vins* (wine list).

WHERE TO EAT

The following constitute only a very small selection of eating places worth trying in this food-loving city. The focus is on Catalan and Mediterranean cuisine and seafood. The star ratings are guidelines and refer to an average à la carte meal per person. The set lunch (including drink of wine, beer, water or soft drink) offered by most restaurants is usually much cheaper.

*	Less than €30
**	€31–46
***	€47–76

Catalan

7 Portes**
Founded in 1836, a true classic. One of the best places for rice dishes. Booking essential.
Pg Isabel II 14 (Barceloneta).
Tel: 93 319 30 33.

Agut*
Dating from the 1920s, this place is typical Barcelona. For a really hearty meal and Catalan 'gastronomic monuments' such as cod with grilled peppers and garlic sauce.
Gignàs 16 (Barri Gòtic).
Tel: 93 315 17 09.

Can Culleretes*
Founded in 1785, full of character, plastered with old photos of famous visitors. Long menu of robust traditional dishes (wild boar, goose and so on), as well as a lighter seafood menu. Very inexpensive set lunches on weekdays, very popular, very crowded.
Quintana 5 (Barri Gòtic).
Tel: 93 317 30 22.

A typical *mar i montanya* dish, chicken with seafood

El Glop*
Informal, homely, slightly rustic air.
Booking recommended.
Sant Lluis 24 (Gràcia). Tel: 93 213 70 58.

El Pa i Trago**
Typical Catalan fare in convivial
atmosphere: red-and-white checked
tablecloths, farm-implement décor
and convivial atmosphere.
Parlament 41 (Sant Antoni).
Tel: 93 441 13 20.

Via Veneto***
Catalan cuisine with fresh market
produce. One of Barcelona's premier
restaurants.
Booking recommended.
Ganduxer 10 (Les Corts).
Tel: 93 200 72 44.

Creative
Appetitus*
Original dishes at reasonable prices.
Very pleasant.
Paris 162 (Eixample). Tel: 93 419 49 33.

The Mediterranean terrace café is a wonderful
invention in a medieval square...

Iposa*
Brilliant for really tight budgets.
Wide range of interesting dishes with
international inspiration, including
vegetarian. Tables by the gardens
behind the Boqueria market.
Floristes de la Rambla 14 (Raval).
Tel: 93 318 60 86.

Jaume de Provença***
Creative chef Jaume Barguès enjoys well-
earned prestige for his original variations
on traditional Catalan cuisine with the
finest quality ingredients. Gourmet
menu offered. Booking essential.
Provença 88 (Eixample).
Tel: 93 430 00 29.

Semproniana*
A whimsical break from style and design,
with its non-matching furniture and
ceramic plates, spectacular old chandeliers
and other flea-market finds. Inventive and
delicious food at reasonable prices. The
star of the dessert menu is the pure
chocolate Delirium Tremens.
Rosselló 148 (Eixample).
Tel: 93 453 18 20.

Seafood
Botafumeiro***
An institution and the very peak of
sophistication for Galician cuisine. Huge
variety of the choicest, freshest seafood,
rice and noodle dishes and sumptuous
bar. Classy and worth every euro.
Gran de Gràcia 81 (Gràcia).
Tel: 93 218 42 30/932 17 96 42.

Can Costa**
Genuine fish and seafood cuisine,
excellent paella and squid. Sunny terrace

...or on the waterfront

with sparkling view over the Port Vell.
Pg Joan de Borbó 70 (Barceloneta).
Tel: 93 221 59 03.

La Oca Mar*
Located right at the tip of the
breakwater, this ship-shaped restaurant
has all-round views of the Med.
Excellent seafood and *cuina de mercat.*
Nova Mar Bella, Espigó Bac de Roda
(Poblenou/Seafront). Tel: 93 225 01 00.

Suquet de l'Almirall**
One of the most interesting seafood
restaurants, blending tradition and
innovation. Perfectly prepared paella, or
try a selection of mini portions of the
chef's suggestions. One of the best wine
cellars in town. Booking recommended.
Passeig Joan de Borbó 65 (Barceloneta).
Tel: 93 221 62 33.

Xiringuito Escribà**
Looks right out over the beach, with
sunny terrace. Delicious fish dishes,
and one of the city's best dessert
selections from the famed Escribà
patissier family.
Av Ronda Litoral 42 (Beach).
Tel: 93 221 07 29.

Mediterranean
Nao Colon**
Near the waterfront, delicious
Mediterranean cuisine with Italian,
French, Catalan and North African
influences. Music at night.
Av Marquès de l'Argentera 19 (El Born).
Tel: 93 268 76 33.

La Provenza*
Much celebrated for imaginative
Mediterranean cuisine with lots of fresh

The Plaça Sant Josep Oriol is a favourite for coffee or an evening drink

vegetables, fish and wonderful sorbets. Booking recommended.
Provença 242 (Eixample).
Tel: 93 323 23 67.

Tragaluz★★

Savour the freshest of Mediterranean ingredients combined in amazingly inventive ways. The place is bathed in light from the glass roof (this is what the name means). Designed by Olympic whizzo Mariscal. Booking essential.
Ptge de la Concepció 5 (Eixample).
Tel: 93 487 06 21.

Cuina de mercat
Bilbao★★

Authentic Mediterranean diet and atmosphere. Well-loved local favourite serving whatever is in season, fresh and simply cooked in traditional style. Home-made desserts and very good wine list.
Perill 33 (Gràcia). Tel: 93 458 96 24.

Can Jaume★

A century-old tavern cheerfully offering cheap traditional fare in an otherwise terribly upmarket street.
Pau Casals 10 (Sarrià–Sant Gervasi).
Tel: 93 200 75 12.

Special settings
Flash Flash★

Unique 1960s-looking place specialising in *tortillas* (omelettes) with every conceivable filling. Never closes.
La Granada del Penedès 25 (Gràcia).
Tel: 93 237 09 90.

Fundació Miró★

Eat international while enjoying panoramic views of the city and contemporary sculpture in the adjoining garden.
Fundació Joan Miró (Montjuïc).
Tel: 93 329 07 68.

L'Hivernacle★

The romantic 19th-century iron and glass tropical plant house is a truly delightful place for a drink, snack or meal.
Passeig de Picasso (Parc de la Ciutadella).
Tel: 93 295 40 17.

La Llotja de les Drassanes★★

Eat well in this superb 13th-century building, in an ambience of art and classical music.
Museu Marítim, Av de les Drassanes (Raval). Tel: 93 302 64 02.

La Venta★★

For a breath of mountain air, lovely terrace and imaginative Catalan-French cuisine.

Plaça Dr Andreu 1 (Tibidabo).
Tel: 93 212 64 55.

Vegetarian
Comme-Bio*
The vegetarian's paradise. With
ecological wines.
Gran Via de les Corts Catalanes 603
(Eixample). Tel: 93 301 03 76.

Juicy Jones*
Very full set menu. Excellent vegan food
with fresh market produce, worldwide
influences.
Cardenal Casañas 7 (Barri Gòtic).
Tel: 93 302 43 30.

Tapas
De Tapa Madre*
The highest quality ingredients make
this one of the city's most popular tapas
bars. Also Castilian 'market' cuisine.
Fresh juices for breakfast, sunny
pavement tables.
Mallorca 301 (Eixample).
Tel: 93 459 31 34.

La Gran Bodega*
For an authentic tapas experience
untouched by trendiness. Thousands
of tapas and authentic décor.
València 193 (Eixample).
Tel: 93 453 10 53.

Pastisseries
Escribà*
Barcelona's monumental *modernista*
pastry shop and café. Gorge on the locally
renowned patissier family's sandwiches
and canapés, cakes and chocolates amidst
mosaics and floral décor.
La Rambla 83 (Liceu). Tel: 93 301 60 27.

Mauri*
An all-time favourite for afternoon tea:
staggering array of canapés, dainty
sandwiches.
Rambla Catalunya 102 (Eixample).
Tel: 93 215 10 20.

Drinks
Boadas*
Barcelona's oldest cocktail bar, founded
in 1933 by the father of the present
owner who brought his cocktail-mixing
skills from Cuba. Unique atmosphere
for a pre- or post-dinner drink. Try the
mojito, Hemingway's favourite.
Tallers 1 (Rambla). Tel: 93 318 88 26.

La Vinya del Señor*
One of the few places where you can try
different wines by the glass, along with

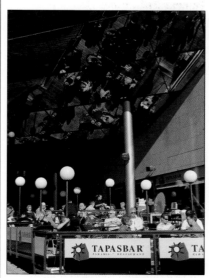

Pause for a snack in the middle of the harbour
in the Maremagnum complex

tiny snacks like olives and slivers of the finest Iberian ham.
Plaça Santa Maria 5 (Barri Gòtic).
Tel: 933 10 33 79.

GOOD THINGS TO BUY

For picnicking, what more could you want than a Mediterranean ploughman's lunch: fresh bread, a selection of olives and cheese, washed down with red wine? There's fresh fruit on sale everywhere all year round, too. Or gorge on real ice cream from a branch of Dino's (*see below*): they sell scores of flavours and will pack your selection into a take-away isothermic container.

For taking home, possibly the first things that spring to mind are virgin olive oil, wine, *cava, moscatel* and *conyac* – look out for Pedrera-chimney-shaped bottles at classy grocers. But if your luggage space is limited there are many other excellent vacuum-packed foods which take up minimal room – *serrano* ham, sausages (*chorizo, llonganissa*), Mallorcan *sobrasada* and even salt cod. Nuts, herbs and handmade chocolates are also good buys. Look out for hexagonal chocolate Gaudí tiles.

Around Christmas time, a delicious easy-to-pack gift is the festive sweet *turrón*. Go for the real artisanal stuff at a reputable pastry shop. Or how about the 'signature' *aceites aromáticos* (aromatic oil) by chef Ferran Adrià (*see pp38–9*) and the Borges company, for sprinkling on food or creating tangy new sauces?

If you can carry heavy parcels home, treat yourself to an earthenware cooking pot or a cast-iron *plantxa* so you can reproduce some of the healthiest food in the world. Fascinating but fragile are glass cruets with the vinegar container, sometimes shaped like a bunch of grapes, inside the oil container. While design supremos like Vinçon sell stylish utensils, the old shops in Gràcia like Soriano's (*see below*) can turn up some gems.

Where to shop for food
Casa del Bacalao
The 'house of cod' sells salted and dried cod with no additives. This is the place to buy the raw material to take home: they will vacuum-pack it for you.
Comtal 8 (Barri Gòtic).

Casa Gispert
Wonderland of nuts, dried fruit and coffee.
Sombrerers 23 (Barri Gòtic).

Colmado Quílez
Wonderful grocery store, a monument in itself: walls lined from floor to ceiling with cans and bottles from the five continents, hams, cheeses, alcohol and *cava*. Mouthwatering.
Rambla de Catalunya 63 (Eixample).

Dino
Traditionally made ice cream in myriad flavours.
Pg Gràcia 33, Pg Gràcia 4, Rambla 54, Pg Juan de Borbón 23.

Ferreteria Soriano
Wonderful old-fashioned store selling traditional utensils like earthenware dishes, special plates for turning Spanish omelettes, drinking flasks, wineskins, asparagus baskets, paella pans and cruet sets.
Gran de Gràcia 53 (Gràcia).

Foix de Sarrià

Not far from Pedralbes monastery, one of the most select pastry shops in town, hushed and reverential, with the added distinction of belonging to the family of the famous Catalan poet JV Foix. Famous for *petxines de Sarrià* (Sarrià shells) made of almond and bitter chocolate.
Pl de Sarrià 12–13 (Sarrià).

Formatgeria La Seu

The Scottish owner of this lovely shop in the old city combs the farmhouses and monasteries of Spain for the best artisan cheeses, which you can taste before buying. Extra-virgin olive oil and Catalan quince also sold.
Dagueria 16 (Barri Gòtic).

L'Illa

Stylish food (and other) shopping in the unmistakeable 'recumbent skyscraper' uptown. This light and airy commercial centre has a typically Mediterranean food market, lots of lovely little stalls, coffee bars and eateries, and a huge branch of the quality Caprabo supermarket. Not as crowded as more central stores.
Av Diagonal 545.

Mel Viadiu

Specialises entirely in honey from different regions of Spain.
Comtal 20 (Barri Gòtic).

J. Murrià

Modernista delicatessen with painted glass frontage and original tiled decoration by Ramón Casas, run by the third generation of the Murrià family. Stocks an impressive range of cured meats, local and European cheeses and hundreds of wines. Men in striped smocks give impeccable old-style service.
Roger de Llúria 85 (Eixample).

VilaViniteca

Thousands of brands of wine and spirits.
Agullers 7 (Barri Gòtic).

TURRÓN

The translation 'nougat' does not do justice to *turrón*, the traditional sweetmeat eaten in every Spanish home at Christmas time. The classic soft Jijona and hard Alicante are both made of almonds, pure honey and sugar. Other mouth-watering varieties are *yema* (egg yolk), *a la piedra* (with lemon peel and cinnamon), coconut, marzipan with crystallised fruits, walnut cream, and chocolate truffle. It is healthy too: rich in calcium, iron and unsaturated vegetable fats and cholesterol-free. For Alicante and Jijona look for the *Denominación Geográfica Específica* seal.

New creative twists to traditional Catalan cooking

Tapas

Tapas – the snacks served with drinks in Spanish bars – are now an internationally popular feature of Spanish eating. These tasty morsels are the perfect appetiser, and most restaurants will give you a dish of olives (or possibly herb-marinated garlic cloves) to nibble on while you sip your drink and await your first course.

Tapas are the fastest of fast food, and you can literally make a meal of them. The ingredients and combinations that go into the making of tapas are limitless. Vegetables, seafood, poultry, dairy products and meat are all pressed into service. They can be served hot or cold or at room temperature. Wonderfully varied, they can be a simple dish of almonds or olives (of which there are numerous types), tiny fried fish, clams, cockles, mussels, sardines, Russian salad, bite-sized squares of potato omelette, tiny earthenware dishes of squid or prawns sizzling in garlic and oil, chicken or salt-cod croquettes. The visual display is mouthwatering but the whole point is that you can try a bit of everything instead of agonising over a menu.

The word *tapa* means a lid or a cover, and tapas were originally pieces of bread or cured ham placed on top of a wine glass to keep dust and flies out. Now they are served everywhere – in homes, village taverns, city bars and upmarket restaurants – but they have kept the informal spirit of their popular origins.

They perform the twofold function of helping to spin drinks out without getting drunk and of provoking thirst. And for the highly social Spaniards, having a drink means conversing, and tapas do not interrupt the flow.

Tapas of course vary according to the taste and traditions of each region, and in fact are not native to Barcelona. Most bars in the city serve a standard selection, although recently several Basque bars which offer a much greater selection have become very popular. Catalonia's appetiser-cum-snack-cum-fast food par excellence, the one which Catalans particularly yearn for when abroad, is *pa amb tomàquet* (bread with tomato): a large slice (*llesca*) of fresh country bread rubbed with the cut side of a ripe tomato, drizzled with virgin olive oil and served with a wide variety of toppings. In fact in Catalunya most sandwiches (except the toasted ham and cheese *bikinis*) are usually made with *tomàquet*.

The local equivalent of the tapas bar is the *llesqueria*. The bread is usually toasted, when it is known as a *torrada*, and is popularly topped with Iberian cured ham (from acorn-fed black-footed pigs), slices of spicy sausage like *chorizo*, *llonganissa* or *fuet*, anchovies or cheese (*formatge*).

Opposite: Several tapas can turn into a whole meal
Above: The waterfront in Barceloneta is lined with restaurants

Hotels and Accommodation

Such is the popularity of Barcelona as a tourist destination, business and conference centre that finding accommodation can be a problem. Billboards on construction sites or gutted buildings all over the city proclaim the imminent opening of 3-, 4- or 5-star hotels to answer this need. Between 1998 and 2002 4,400 new rooms were available and in 2003 alone nearly 3,000 more. Even so when a Trade Fair coincides with a Festival of Advanced Music in a month when holidaymakers are passing through, it is virtually impossible to find a room.

The awesome Arts Hotel, a favourite for rock stars

As a result, prices are high. Hotels are categorised from 1-star to 5-star and even 5-star GL (*Gran Luxe*), but the pricing policy is liberal, so market conditions call the tune. Standards at the lower end of the hotel scale have been forced to improve over the last few years but these establishments are sought after and quite highly priced anywhere near the centre. *Pensions* are categorised from 1 to 2 stars. They range from pretty basic with no external window to clean, homely rooms with a view. Visitors are turning to alternatives, such as self-catering apartments or bed and breakfast, which are proliferating in the city. A good agency is BCNrooms (*Tel: 93 226 54 67. www.bcnrooms.com*).

With this scenario it is obviously important to book early – or check whether your dates coincide with a peak period before booking flights. There are innumerable sites on the Internet, but the more official ones are through the city website *www.bcn.es* or the tourist office website *www.barcelonaturisme.com*. The Generalitat site at *www.gencat.es/probert* has a good tourist section for the whole of Catalonia, including the capital. The excellent tourist information office below ground in Plaça Catalunya has a last-minute booking service (*Plaça Catalunya 17-S. Open: daily 9am–9pm*), as does their office in the airport and in the Montseny service station on the A7 (E15) *autopista*, the motorway coming down from France (*Area de servei Montseny-Sud, km117*). For youth hostels and cheaper accommodation try *www.europeanhostels.com* or *www.catalunya.co.uk*.

Prices

The guide prices here are based on a typical double room, including tax but not normally breakfast.

*	Less than €50
**	€50–100

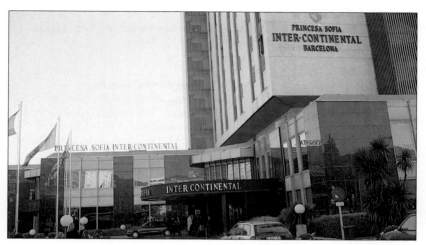

Several international chain hotels are located on the upper part of the Avinguda Diagonal

★★★	€100–150
★★★★	€150–250
★★★★★	over €250

★★★★★

Hotel Arts Barcelona
Utter glamour in this 42-storey luxurious hotel looking over the Olympic Port where the rich, famous and beautiful stay.
Marina 19–21. Tel: 93 221 10 00.

Hotel Claris
Nouveau luxury and very slick behind the façade of a former palace.
Swimming pool and bar on roof.
Pau Claris 150. Tel: 93 487 62 62.

Gran Hotel Florida
After a glorious past with guests like Hemingway and James Stewart this has just reopened as the city's first 5-star Relais Château. On the hill of Tibidabo with stunning views and prices.

Carretera Vallvidrera a Tibidabo 83–89. Tel: 93 259 30 00.

Hotel Ritz
Everything a Ritz should be, plush and comfortable with old-world atmosphere. Dalí had a retainer on the Royal Suite for years. Sunken Roman baths in the suites.
Gran Via de les Corts Catalanes 668. Tel: 93 318 52 00. www.ritzbcn.com.

★★★★

Hotel Albinoni
The hotel has some restored artefacts from Rocamora palace. Very charming décor and in good position between Gothic quarter and Eixample.
Avinguda Portal de l'Angel 17. Tel: 93 318 41 41. www.hoteles-catalonia.es.

Hotel Duques de Bergara

Beautiful *modernista* entrance to this former 19th-century town house just off Plaça Catalunya. Tastefully done right down to the lap pool in the inner courtyard.
Bergara 11. Tel: 93 301 51 51.

★★★

Citadines Apart'Hotel

Good value self-catering studios and apartments an olive-stone's throw from the Boqueria market.
La Rambla 122. Tel: 93 270 11 11.

Hotel Granvía

Old-fashioned gem just off Passeig de Gràcia, a rare discovery.
Gran Vía de les Corts Catalanes 642. Tel: 93 318 19 00.

Park Hotel

Original '50s décor stylishly restored in this low-key attractive hotel near

Ciutadella Park.
Avinguda Marquès de l'Argentera 11. Tel: 93 319 60 00.

★★

Hotel Banys Orientals

Good-looking new hotel near the Born. Possibly the best value in town.
Argenteria 37. Tel: 93 268 84 60.

Hotel Continental

Eccentric, family-run hotel in prime spot. Ask for a room with a balcony on La Rambla.
La Rambla 138. Tel: 93 301 25 70. www.hotelcontinental.com.

Hotel Espanya

Breakfast among the extravagant ceramic tiles and painted mermaids of Domènech i Montaner, who renovated this good-value hotel in 1900.
Sant Pau 9–11. Tel: 93 318 17 58.

After recent refurbishment the Ritz has recovered its former glory

Hotel Ginebra

Good price for excellent position.
Request room overlooking Plaça
Catalunya.
Rambla de Catalunya 1, 3º.
Tel: 93 317 10 63.

Hotel Jardí

Much sought-after for its position
overlooking two squares in the heart
of the Gothic quarter. Book well in
advance and demand an exterior room.
Plaça Sant Josep Oriol 1.
Tel: 93 301 59 00.

Hostal-Residencia Windsor

Amazing value in one of the finest
streets in the Eixample. Only 15 rooms
so book early. Request room 106, the
one with a 19th-century bay window.
Rambla de Catalunya 84.
Tel: 93 215 11 98.

*

Kabul

Youth hostel in magnificent square.
Plaça Reial 17. Tel: 93 318 51 90.

Pension Ciudadela

Reasonable rooms in a great position
near Ciutadella Park and port.
Commercio 33, 1º,1ª. Tel: 93 319 62 03.

Pension Teruel

Impeccably clean and luminous on an
attractive square just off La Rambla in
very central spot.
Plaça Bonsuccés 6, 3º.
Tel: 93 302 61 20.

The Gran Hotel Havana, a modern interior
within the original Eixample façade

FORUM 2004

The building work is accelerating with the
imminence of the Forum 2004 and its
expected 5 million visitors. Some 20 new
hotels will offer another 3,500 rooms. By the
end of 2005 there will be twelve new hotels in
the new Diagonal Mar area. What is on offer
is becoming more interesting: hotels looking
right over the beach, a luxury hotel where
Hemingway used to stay brought back to
life, one in the Casa Fuster, a Domènech i
Montaner *modernista* building, a designer
hotel run by trendy restaurant owners. With
early booking there is no need to be
condemned to an impersonal chain hotel.

Practical Guide

Arriving
Formalities

A valid passport is necessary to enter Spain. EU nationals (except from the Republic of Ireland or Denmark) can in theory use an identity card and do not require visas, but it still seems to be a grey area so it is recommended to bring a passport. If you intend to stay more than 90 days you should, by law, report to the police. If you are a citizen of the USA, Canada, Australia or New Zealand you need a visa if you intend to stay longer than 90 days. It is advisable to check with your consulate before leaving home as entry regulations are always liable to change. For other nationalities it is getting increasingly difficult to enter so be sure to check before travelling.

By Air

National and international flights fly to Barcelona's airport, **El Prat**. An air shuttle connects Barcelona with Madrid and there are regular flights to the major regional capitals. The national airline

A tourist bus is a good option for getting an overall idea of the place

Iberia and its affiliate **Aviaco** operate most domestic air routes. International flights use either terminal A or B, and it is important to establish which your return flight will depart from.

There are several budget airlines flying to Barcelona from European cities, including EasyJet, Basiq Air and Sterling. These all offer great deals if you can be flexible with travel plans. Ryanair is expanding its schedule to Girona Airport, which is only an hour away from Barcelona by shuttle bus.

Barcelona centre is 12km from El Prat airport. The easiest way in is on the *Aerobús*, which leaves each terminal every 15 minutes and stops in Plaça Espanya, Plaça Universitat and ends in Plaça Catalunya, from 5.30am to midnight. The fare is about €4. There is also a train service which goes through Sants, Plaça Catalunya and Arc de Triomf before going on up the Maresme coast to Mataró.

You may have to queue longer for a taxi than for a bus, but the ride will only take about 20–25 minutes to the centre. Taxis are entitled to charge a supplement from the airport and for luggage. The fare is about €20.
El Prat Airport. Tel: 93 298 38 38.
Iberia. Tel: 020 7830 0011 (UK), 902 40 05 00 (Spain). www.iberia.es.

By Road

There is a good motorway, the A7 (also known as E15) covering the 160km from La Jonquera on the French border to Barcelona. The tolls amount to €10. In the service stations try to park where there is a security guard. The motorway links continue to Lleida, Madrid and Valencia. The ring road around Barcelona can become congested at peak times but is basically efficient: Ronda Litoral is the coastal part, good for the seafront and Old Town, while Ronda de Dalt is the mountain side, better for the uptown districts. For the Eixample it is often best to follow signs to Avinguda Meridiana.

By Coach

There are good services linking Barcelona with most other cities in Spain at reasonable prices, from either Estació d'Autobusos Sants (*tel: 93 490 40 00*) or Estació de Nord (*tel: 93 265 65 08*), a smart coach station in the former railway station. International lines Julià, Eurolines and Linebús run into both stations.

By Rail

Mainline trains to and from Barcelona – international, national, regional and local (*Cercanías*) – are operated by the state-owned company **RENFE** (Red Nacional de Ferrocarriles). The Catalan government-run network known as FGC (*Ferrocarrils de la Generalitat de Catalunya*) offers a good suburban service, covering the up-town districts of the city and some of the smaller towns beyond, including the Collserola hills.
RENFE. Tel: 902 24 02 02.
www.renfe.es. For international lines tel: 902 24 34 02. RENFE has no agent in the UK but Rail Europe (tel: 020 7647 49 00) can supply some types of ticket.
FGC. Tel: 93 205 15 15. www.fgc.net.

Barcelona metro

Camping

There are several options for camping south of Barcelona in Castelldefels, or on the Costa Maresme to the north. Information from Catalan tourism. *Tel: 93 238 40 00. www.gencat.es/probert.*

Children

Children under four travel free on public transport. Those under 18 will get free admission into some national museums but they will have to pay in private ones – although sometimes there are reductions for the under-12s. *See pp160–61.*

Climate

See p5.

BARCELONA

Average Rainfall for year 63mm (2.5in)
Average Temperature for year 16°C/61°F

Weather Conversion Chart
25.4mm = 1 inch
°F = 1.8 x °C + 32

Crime

Barcelona, like most cities, is not free from petty crime – but most is opportunist and easily prevented if you take the obvious precautions. Watch out for pickpockets and bag snatchers in crowded places like the airport, stations and metro, as well as bars and terraces. Be careful in the narrow streets of the Old Town and particularly on La Rambla, where distracted by one of the performers you become a sitting target. Bags and cameras should be worn across your chest and in front of you, and money belts hidden. Never carry valuables with you and never leave anything in a car. Items of value are best stored in a hotel safe. Avoid walking alone at night in poorly lit areas and get a taxi if you can. When driving keep doors locked and ignore people offering to help you at traffic lights. If you are unlucky enough to be robbed, report it immediately to the police (*Policia Nacional*) by making a statement (*denuncia*) in the police station (*comisaría*). This is essential for insurance purposes.

Customs Regulations

You can bring into Spain, free of duty, all personal belongings and 800 cigarettes or 200 cigars; 10 litres of spirits and 90 litres of wine; 20 litres of fortified wine; 110 litres of beer; 60ccl of perfume and 250ccl of toilet water. You can take as much money as you want into Spain.

Driving

The best advice about driving is do not. Barcelona traffic moves very fast in several lanes. Woe betide any driver trying to study a map, or attempting to move across lanes of traffic to turn left or right. Local drivers show no mercy and the horn blowing will test the calmest nerves. Parking is difficult and expensive, and if you have to recover an illegally parked car from the police compound it is exorbitant. If you do choose to arrive by car it is best to leave it in a car park and use the excellent public transport system.

The ring roads and motorways (*autopistas*) out of Barcelona are efficient, but do get very crowded at peak times, especially on Friday and Sunday evenings.

Breakdown

If you have a breakdown you can contact the **Dirección General de Tráfico, Asistencia en Carreteras** (*tel: 90 012 35 05*). There are SOS telephones along the motorways. Your own travel insurance should include an emergency number.

Car Hire

All the major car-hire companies have offices in the centre of Barcelona as well as at the airport. Rates are competitive but you can usually get the best deal by reserving a car from home at the same time as making a flight booking. When hiring a car you will be asked to show your passport and EU or international driving licence. It is worth paying a little extra for a car with air-conditioning if you are travelling between June and September.

Some of the main companies are **Avis** (*tel: 902 13 55 31. www.avis.es*); **Europcar**

Catch taxis at a rank or on any street corner

(*tel: 902 10 50 30. www.europcar.es*); **Hertz** (*tel: 902 40 24 05. www.hertz.es*); **National/Atesa** (*tel: 902 10 01 01. www.atesa.es*); **Vanguard** (*tel: 93 439 38 80. www.vanguardrent.com*). A good local company is **Over** (*tel: 90 241 04 10*). If you book well in advance or off-season, **EasyCar** prices are hard to beat, but it is essential to play by their rules and read the small print to avoid nasty extras added to your final account (*www.easycar.com*). The other problem is that because of their exterior publicity stickers you are easily spotted as a vulnerable tourist and good for robberies. There are three branches in Barcelona.

Documents and Insurance

In Spain you are obliged by law to carry your passport with you all the time in case the police ask for identification. The same applies to your driving licence and your car papers if you are driving. Most national driving licences are valid but it is advisable to have an international driving licence. In your car you must carry a red warning triangle and replacement light bulbs.

Fuel

Petrol (*gasolina*) is available as *super*, *normal* (both leaded), *sin plomo* (unleaded) and *gasoil* (diesel).

Traffic Regulations

Spain drives on the right and its highway code is similar to that of other European countries, with internationally recognised traffic signs. Warning: the police can issue on-the-spot fines for traffic offences, and being a foreigner does not give you exemption. If you have not got the cash they will offer to drive you to the nearest cash machine. Seat-belts are obligatory and children under 12 should travel in the back. Speed limits are 120 km/h on motorways, 100 km/h on other roads and 50km/h in built-up areas. It is forbidden to drive under the influence of alcohol.

Electricity

Although Spain's electricity supply is 220 volts, you may find 125 volts in some old buildings. All plugs in Spain have only two round pins so if you are bringing any electrical appliance from the UK make sure you have an adapter for it.

Embassies

Most embassies are in Madrid, and in Barcelona there are consulates.

Australia
Gran Via Carles III 98. Tel: 93 330 94 96.
Canada
Elisenda de Pinós 10. Tel: 93 204 27 00.
Ireland
Gran Via Carles III 94. Tel: 93 491 50 21.
UK
Avinguda Diagonal 477.
Tel: 93 366 62 00.

USA
Passeig Reina Elisenda 23.
Tel: 93 280 22 27.

Emergency Telephone Numbers

If you have an emergency anywhere in Spain and need the police, the fire brigade or an ambulance dial **112** and ask for the service you require. In Barcelona the following numbers also apply:

Ambulance (*Ambulancia*): 112
Doctor (emergency service): 061
Fire brigade (*Bomberos*): 080 or 112
Guardia Urbana: 092
Police (*Policía Nacional*): 091 or 112
General information (about the city): 010
General information (about Catalonia): 012
Public transport: 010

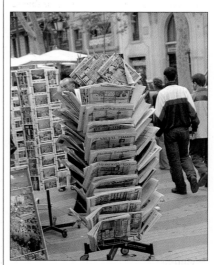

Newspapers and magazines from around the world in La Rambla news-stands

The Thomas Cook Worldwide Customer Promise offers free emergency assistance at any Thomas Cook Network travel location to travellers who have purchased their travel tickets at a Thomas Cook location. Report (within 24 hours) the loss or theft of Thomas Cook Traveller's Cheques, using their 24-hour reverse-charge telephone number:
00 44 1733 318950.

Health
British citizens – as all EU nationals – are entitled to treatment from the Spanish public health system, known as social security. Obtain the relevant form before travelling. UK citizens need an E111 form, available from post offices. If you need medical attention you will have to show this form to the doctor. Note, however, that not all treatments are covered by the E111 and it is advisable to have private medical insurance as well. If you are a US citizen you should check with your insurer before you leave home to see if you are covered in the EU.

If you need an emergency doctor tell the hotel reception or go directly to *Urgencies* in the nearest hospital. The **Hospital Clinic** has a good reputation, though you may have to wait for a long time. Alternatively go to a private clinic like the Teknon, or contact your embassy or consulate. If you need hospital treatment always ask for an itemised bill in case you need it for your insurance. You do not need vaccinations to enter Spain.

Chemists
There is always a 24-hour chemist (*farmácia de guardia*) open in each neighbourhood. The name and address of the one on duty will be hanging in the entrance to any chemist. It is common to consult the pharmacist for the most suitable medication in the case of minor ailments. There are still plenty of herbalists around, especially in the Old Town.

Insurance
It is always advisable to take out personal travel insurance before travelling. This can be obtained from your travel agent, tour operator or any insurance company. Make sure it gives adequate cover for medical expenses, loss or theft, personal liability and repatriation. If you are driving check with your insurer on your cover for damage, loss or theft of the vehicle and for liability. And make sure you have a green card.

If you hire a car you will probably have to pay for collision insurance. Check with your insurers as you may already be covered for this on overseas hires.

Lost Property
If you lose anything you must report it to the police in your nearest police station (*comisaría*) because you will need the report to make an insurance claim. If you lose an important document such as your passport you must also report it to your consulate who can issue a temporary passport. If you lose your traveller's cheques, contact the issuing company. For lost and found items go to the lost property office, **Oficina de Troballes**. *Carrer Ciutat 9. Tel: 906 42 70 17. Open: 9.30am–1pm.*

LANGUAGE

An attempt to speak Catalan will win hearts, but if you have a little Spanish and want to practise it, very few people will mind. Try to speak one of the two, though, rather than just bulldozing on in loud English!

Some useful phrases in both official languages

English	Catalan	Spanish
Yes	si	sí
No	no	no
Please	si us plau	por favor
Sorry	perdoni	perdone
Thank you	gràcies	gracias
Bon appetit	bon profit	buen provecho
Hello	hola	hola
Goodbye	adéu	adiós
Morning	matí	mañana
Good morning	bon dia	buenos días
Afternoon/evening	tarda	tarde
Good afternoon/evening	bona tarda	buenas tardes
Night	nit	noche
Good night	bona nit	buenas noches
Where is...?	¿On està...?	¿Donde está...?
How much is...?	¿quant val...?	¿Cuánto cuesta...?
Breakfast	esmorzar	desayuno
Lunch	dinar	almuerzo
Dinner	sopar	cena
Open	obert	abierto
Closed	tancat	cerrado

Days of the week

Monday	dilluns	lunes
Tuesday	dimarts	martes
Wednesday	dimecres	miércoles
Thursday	dijous	jueves
Friday	divendres	viernes
Saturday	dissabte	sábado
Sunday	diumenge	domingo

Maps

Maps of the city can be obtained from the tourist offices. The official one sold for under €2 is excellent, with useful information on its reverse side. The newspaper stands on La Rambla have a good selection of maps of Catalonia and the rest of Spain.

Media

European and American newspapers like *The International Herald Tribune*, *The Financial Times* and *The Guardian Europe* are easily found in the newspaper stands on La Rambla. FNAC in Plaça Catalunya has a huge magazine section on the ground floor. Many hotels have satellite TV with programmes in English. The state-owned Spanish television network has two main channels, TV1 and TV2. Catalan television is of a good standard with two channels, TV3 and Canal 33, and children's programmes from 5 to 8pm. Barcelona TV is a new channel focussed on what is happening in the city, with some information in English during summer months.

Metropolitan is an informative monthly magazine published in English, available free from bookshops, cafés and the Palau de la Virreina information centre at *La Rambla 99*.

Money Matters
Currency

In Spain, as in most of the EU, the currency is the euro. It is divided into 100 *centimos*. There are coins of 1 and 2 euros and of 1, 2, 5, 10, 20 and 50 *centimos*. The notes are of 5, 10, 20, 50, 100, 200 and 500 euros.

Nearly every bank has 24-hour automatic cash machines

Banks

Banks are usually open to the public from 8.30am to 2pm Monday to Friday and on Saturday in the winter months from 8.30am to 1pm. In Catalonia the savings banks like La Caixa or Caixa de Catalunya function just like banks but are closed on Saturdays. Most banks and savings banks have cash machines. Traveller's cheques can be cashed in the main hotels and in bureaux de change, though the rate may be more favourable in banks. There is a Caixa de Catalunya bank for changing money in the tourist information office in Plaça Catalunya, *open Mon–Sat 9am–9pm, Sun (in summer) 9am–2pm*.

Credit Cards

Major credit cards are accepted in hotels, shops and most restaurants. However smaller *pensions*, local restaurants, bars and shops will not accept them. Shops request passport or some personal identity to purchase with credit card, however small the amount. Personal cheques are not usually accepted anywhere in Spain.

Opening Hours

Markets open at 8am. Supermarkets are generally open from 9am to 1.30 or 2pm and from 5pm to 8pm Monday to Saturday. The larger supermarkets stay open through lunch. Department stores and the chain fashion shops usually open at 10am but stay open until 9 or 10pm. The smaller ones close at lunchtime. Museums, galleries and public buildings often close on Monday but their timetables are variable (*see pp134–7*).

Police

The Spanish police is divided into three forces: *Policía Nacional* who deal mainly with national security, crime, terrorism, residency documents and work permits; *Policía Municipal* or *Guàrdia Urbana*

Euros have been standard currency since 2002

who deal mainly with traffic regulations, fines and crime in local communities; and the *Guàrdia Civil*, a paramilitary body who normally police rural areas but who also control the borders, highways and state buildings and take part in anti-terrorist operations. Their uniform is green. Catalunya has its own police force, the *Mossos d'Esquadra*, who are gradually taking over responsibility from the national police, especially outside Barcelona.

The *Guàrdia Urbana* has an office on La Rambla which deals with tourist problems in many languages: *Turisme Atenció, La Rambla 43. Open: 24 hours. Tel: 93 344 13 00.*

Post Offices

There are small post offices (*Correos*) in every district, but the main one is in a magnificent building near the port in Plaça Antoni López. Letters can be weighed and stamps bought from tobacconists (*estancos*) which avoids a lot of queuing.
Main Post Office, Plaça Antoni López. www.correos.es. Open: Mon–Sat 8.30am–9.30pm, Sun 8.30am–2.30pm.

The city police, *Guàrdia Urbana*, occasionally patrol on horseback

Public Holidays

For Catalan feast days and festivals see pp22–3. National public holidays are as follows:

1 January **Año Nuevo** (New Year's Day)
6 January **Día de Reyes** (Epiphany)
Viernes Santo (Good Friday). Variable, March or April. Easter Monday is a holiday in Catalonia.
1 May **Día del Trabajo** (Labour Day)
15 August **La Asunción** (Assumption Day)
12 Octobre **Día de la Hispanidad** (National Day of Spain) known as La Pilar in Catalonia.
1 November **Todos los Santos** (All Saints' Day)
6 December **Día de la Constitución** (Constitution Day)
8 December **Inmaculada Concepción** (Immaculate Conception)
25 December **Día de Navidad** (Christmas Day)

Public Transport

The official tourist bus is a good option for getting orientated. Its two routes interlink and cover the key parts of the city. Purchase your tickets on the bus, which leaves from Plaça Catalunya but can be caught anywhere on the route. *See also pp26–9.*

Telephones

For international calls dial 00 + country code. In Spain all numbers include the regional prefix which must be used even if you are in the same region. So if you dial Barcelona from Madrid the number begins with 93, and if you are in Barcelona you must also dial 93 + number.

The *Metro* underground system is fast, efficient and air-conditioned

Time

Spain follows Central European Time which is Greenwich Mean Time + 1 hour or US Eastern Standard Time + 6 hours.

Tourist Information

The Spanish tourist office in the UK is at *22–23 Manchester Square, London W1M 5AP. Tel: 020 7486 8077. www.tourspain.co.uk; www.tourspain.es.*

The Catalan tourist office is at *17 Fleet Street, London EC4Y 1AA. Tel: 020 7583 8855.*

In Barcelona the main tourist information office is below ground in *Plaça Catalunya 17-S, open daily 9am–9pm.* Also at the airport, Sants and Plaça Sant Jaume. *www.bcn.es* and *www.barcelonaturisme.com* are good web pages.

Travellers with Disabilities

Gradually metro, FGC and mainline train stations are installing lifts. Some of the bus routes have buses with a hydraulic platform. *Tel: 010.*

ACKNOWLEDGEMENTS

Thomas Cook Publishing wishes to thank the photographers, picture libraries and other organisations for the loan of the photographs reproduced in this book, to whom the copyright in the photographs belong.

Ajuntament de Barcelona	21a, 96, 97b
Arnim Schulz	65
Castellers de Barcelona	17
Chris Oliver	4a, 5a, 27a, 79a, 88, 90a, 90b, 92, 93, 98, 108a, 109b, 115, 129, 153
Dewi Williams	119
El Liceu	82, 83
Fototeca.com – E. Casas	120
Fototeca.com – G. Serra I Llimona	131
Guitar Festival of Barcelona	22b
La Paloma Nightclub	76
Mike Merchant	15, 118a, 118b, 126, 127
Neil Setchfield	22a, 30, 51, 56a, 84, 154b, 169
Patronat de Turisme Costa Brava Girona	
F. Guillamet	167
Fons PTCBG	163
Foto Minguell	162a
Ramon Manent. International Gaudi Year	43
Razzmatazz Nightclub	77
Sarah Andrews	14a, 26b, 122b
Turisme de Catalunya, Arxiu Nacional de Catalunya	
Francisco Bedmar	38
Jordi Pareto	5b, 13, 122a, 124a
Marc Rosés	32a
Montserrat Sagarra	18b, 91
Santy Carbonell	142
Vincon	70
www.barcelona2004.org	
Focus	58
Ivo Rovira	154a
Jordi López Dot	100
Infrastructures del Llevant de Barcelona, S.A.	59

The remaining pictures were supplied by Gavin Harrison.